Of Life and Salvation

Reflections on Living the Christian Life

Based on the Fourteen Scripture Readings of
the Orthodox Christian Church's Sacrament of
Holy Unction

Stanley Samuel Harakas

D1603815

LIGHT & LIFE PUBLISHING
Minneapolis, Minnesota

Light and Life Publishing
P.O. Box 26421
Minneapolis, MN 55426-0421

Copyright © 1996
Stanley S. Harakas
Library of Congress No. 96-75603

ISBN 1-880971-17-8

TO

". . . our Lord and Savior Jesus Christ. To him be the glory both now and to the day of eternity. Amen."
(2 Pet. 3:18)

AND TO

Our Grandson
Stephen Constantine DeFilippo

Table of Contents

Of Life and Salvation

The Scripture Readings in the Eastern Orthodox Sacrament of Holy Unction

This book invites you to reflect on the meaning of the fourteen biblical passages that are part of the current text of the Sacrament of Holy Unction. As you will see below, these fourteen passages were deliberately selected to be included in the order of the Church's sacrament of healing.

This deliberate and careful selection has brought together some of the most meaningful and enlightening messages of the New Testament in a single place. They are rich expressions of the revelation of God's will for us, especially those who are members of the household of the faith, that is, the Church.

The Bible in the Life of the Church

In the Orthodox Church's understanding, God has revealed great truths to the world about Himself and humanity, sin and redemption, and right and holy living. He has done this not as an abstract set of ideas, but through His relationship with people. This revelation flows from a living encounter and relationship with God. In the Orthodox teaching, we refer to the witness of this encounter, guided and inspired by the Holy Spirit, as Holy

Tradition, which is preserved and protected by the Church as a living experience.

The Scriptures, the Old and New Testaments, are a central and essential element of Holy Tradition. The writings of Church Fathers and Mothers, the decisions of church councils (especially ecumenical councils), the development of worship and sacramental services, the canons (rules) of the Church, and an intangible, yet real and identifiable mindset, what could be called *the Orthodox Christian ethos,* serve to guide our understanding of Scripture. Holy Tradition and Scripture cannot be separated because the Scriptures are a product of the living encounter with God embodied in Holy Tradition. The Scriptures, in turn, anchor Holy Tradition while Holy Tradition provides the understanding of the meaning of the Scriptures.

The place of the Holy Scriptures in the life of the Orthodox Church is immense. Every service of public worship in the Orthodox Church is permeated with references to the Holy Scriptures. It would be well-nigh impossible to read a page from the writings of the Church Fathers without encountering numerous passages from the Bible. A few minutes with an Orthodox theological study will show you a text filled with biblical passages. Even the canons and rules of the Orthodox Church are frequently formulated to include biblical passages. The Bible is *everywhere* in the Orthodox Church's life!

Holy Unction and Scripture

Just one of these expressions of the life of the Orthodox Church, the Sacrament of Holy Unction or the Sacrament of Prayer Oil, is a case in point. It is based on a passage from the letter of St. James in the New Testament (1:10-16). One of the earliest prayer books of the Church, a fourth-century collection of prayers and services that were in existence in an even earlier time, is known as *The Sacramentary of Serapion.*

The man who compiled this prayer book was named Serapion. He was the bishop of the Egyptian town of Thmius from 339 to 360 A.D. In this work we find two prayers related to the Sacrament of Holy Unction: one is the blessing of the oil; the other is the prayer of anointing. In the first prayer we read:

> . . . we pray Thee to send down from the
> heavens of thy Only-begotten, a curative power
> upon this oil, in order that to those who are
> anointed (with it) . . . it may become a means of
> removing "every disease and every sickness" (Matt.
> 4:23), . . . *a medicine of life and salvation,* unto
> health and soundness of soul and body and spirit,
> unto perfect well-being.

It is from this prayer that the title of this book has been taken: *Of Life and Salvation.* In the first centuries of the Church, the two prayers were added to the Divine Liturgy when the Sacrament of Holy Unction was conducted for someone who was seeking healing of soul and body and spirit.

Concurrently, the monks of the Orthodox Church established what you and I know today as hospitals. Their purpose was to provide medical treatment for the poor who could not afford regular treatment from physicians. By hiring physicians, organizing the practice of medicine in a single place within the confines of their monasteries, serving as administrators, nurses, cooks and maintenance workers, they invented the institution which they called *Xenon* and we have come to call a hospital.

In time, the monks' practice of bringing together physicians contributed not only to the development of medical specialties, but it also fostered the cross-fertilization of medical knowledge. This new development soon made the medicine practiced in the monastery-run hospitals much better than the medicine practiced privately by individual doctors.

This state of affairs lasted from the fifth century to the eleventh century, when the imperial government and the medical guilds of Byzantium took away the administration of the hospitals from the Church and gave control of the hospitals to the physicians. If you would like to read more about these events, you could read my book, *Health and Medicine in the Eastern Orthodox Tradition* now republished by Light and Life Publishing Company.

What happened next is described in that book:

It should not surprise us that the church sought some way of responding to this exclusion from the healing process in the society of that day. In the subsequent century tendencies to enhance the liturgical form of the sacrament of healing led to its separation from the context of the Divine Liturgy and to the formation of a service complete in itself.

....

Nicephorus, patriarch of Constantinople from 1260 to 1261, wrote that his predecessor, Patriarch Arsenius Autoreianus (1255-60), had ordered officially that the sacrament of holy unction be conducted by seven priests, defining also seven prayers to be said during the service. He had also increased the number of biblical readings from two to seven.

Seven Epistle Readings and Seven Gospel Readings

Eventually the seven Scripture readings were increased to fourteen, apparently by Symeon, archbishop of Thessalonica (1410-29), seven epistle readings and seven gospel readings. The selection of the Scripture readings for this sacrament is impressive. Some of the richest, most meaningful, inspiring, challenging, and illuminating passages of the New Testament are included in these fourteen readings.

For Whom Is This Book Written?

These passages are not only rich in references to healing physical and spiritual ills, they are also profound sources for living the Christian life. They are, indeed, "Of Life and Salvation" and they provide us with guidance, direction, and wisdom for our lives in this world and in the world to come. As sources of wisdom and instruction, they are valuable resources for living the Orthodox Christian life.

This is especially true for the people for whom this book is primarily written: those Orthodox Christians seeking to understand the Scriptures from within the Orthodox tradition because they are convinced that the truth of the Lord is necessary for their growth in the Godlike Orthodox Christian life.

Nevertheless, inquirers into the Orthodox Faith, those who have been alienated from it for some reason, non-Orthodox Christians, and nonbelievers are invited to read these reflections, as well. Perhaps the thoughts and insights presented here may help rekindle dormant sparks of faith or restore confidence in the Orthodox way.

The primary audience, however, remains the Orthodox Christian who is seeking to deepen his or her life of faith.

Background and Acknowledgments

These "Reflections" began as a series of monthly articles in the mid-1980s in *The Word* magazine of the Antiochian Orthodox Christian Archdiocese of North America. The series began with the three general reflections presented at the beginning of this book as Preliminary Reflections about Orthodox Church life. They were followed by a series of monthly Biblical Reflections based on the fourteen texts of the Unction Service.

Almost two-thirds of the reflections were published in the *The Word* over a period of a few years. Unfortunately, the series was never finished. Pressures of work, duties as a member of the faculty of Holy Cross Greek Orthodox School of Theology in Brookline, MA, and pastoral responsibilities pushed this effort aside for almost a decade.

In the summer of 1995 my wife Emily and I retired from active service and I turned my attention to the formidable task of completing over a half-dozen unfinished manuscripts. *Of Life and Salvation* is the first fruit of my "life in retirement." It has been published with the permission of the editor of *The Word*, Fr. George S. Corey, whose original encouragement never wavered. When I asked for permission to collect the articles and told him of my intention to finish the reflections for publication in a book, he was very supportive. For this I am very grateful.

The original reflections have been edited for this book; some have been revised; and a few have been extensively revised. The balance of the reflections were written to complete the volume. Please note that I do not provide references to quotations in this book other than for biblical passages. The biblical translation used is the Revised Standard Version of the Bible. Quotations from St. John Chrysostom are taken from the Nicene and Post-Nicene Fathers series, but they have been modernized and in some cases slightly revised for purposes of clarity.

In addition to Fr. George Corey, I also want to thank Fr. Anthony Coniaris of Light and Life Publishing Company for considering this book for publication. He has been a steady inspiration to me over the years.

How To Read This Book

A word about how to read this book. You will notice that some of the readings have one reflection and others have more than one. In each reflection, the tone is one of "instructive conversation." I hope you will read these reflections as if I were seated opposite you and speaking out loud these thoughts about the Orthodox Christian life, based on the rich Scriptural passages provided for us by the Sacrament of Holy Unction.

At the beginning of each Reflection is the biblical passage. Read that first prayerfully, thoughtfully, reflectively. Then read the reflection from beginning to end. You may then want to read each subheading as a starting point for your own reflection. Don't hurry through them. Ask questions about how the teachings and ideas apply to your life. That will make this book what it is intended to be, a conversation between me and you, with the goal of helping you grow in healing past shortcomings, growing toward living the Orthodox Christian way of life, and making your salvation in Christ real.

It would be useful, perhaps, for groups to also use this book in the manner described above. Families might want to use it as a part of their own family spiritual development. Parish priests might try using some or all of the Reflections for parish study groups or Bible classes. In this way the "instructive conversation" might expand the circle of spiritual communion envisaged by this book.

Dear reader, my prayers are with you as we journey together reflecting on these passages from the New Testament, passages which are *Of Life and Salvation!*

Preliminary Reflection 1

Living the Whole Faith
Luke 13:22-30

[22]He went on his way through towns and villages, teaching, and journeying toward Jerusalem. [23]And some one said to him, "Lord, will those who are saved be few?" And he said to them, [24]"Strive to enter by the narrow door; for many, I tell you, will seek to enter and will not be able. [25]When once the householder has risen up and shut the door, you will begin to stand outside and to knock at the door, saying, 'Lord, open to us.' He will answer you, 'I do not know where you come from.' [26]Then you will begin to say, 'We ate and drank in your presence, and you taught in our streets.' [27]But he will say, 'I tell you, I do not know where you come from; depart from me, all you workers of iniquity!' [28]There you will weep and gnash your teeth, when you see Abraham and Isaac and Jacob and all the prophets in the kingdom of God and you yourselves thrust out. [29]And men will come from east and west, and from north and south, and sit at table in the kingdom of God. [30]And behold, some are last who will be first, and some are first who will be last."

Most people like things to be simple. It is so much easier if we can reduce everything to a formula, to a rule, to a motto. That way we don't need to think, we don't need discernment, and life can be neatly put into compartments: religion, family, business, education, etc. It is comforting to do that, but it doesn't really work. Reducing everything in life to a formula nearly always distorts reality and gives us the wrong signals and guidelines for life. This is just as true in the Christian life, especially since the Christian life has to do with our relationship with God and our relationships with our fellow human beings, both within and outside the Church.

A Disturbing Encounter

In the thirteenth chapter of the Gospel of Saint Luke, Jesus seems to be describing what the Kingdom of God is like. Luke's account in chapter 13 emphasizes the Kingdom's quiet, yet sure, growth and development. In verse 18, the Kingdom is compared with a grain of mustard seed, which "*grew and became a tree, and the birds of the air made nests in its branches.*" In the next passage, the Kingdom is compared to the leaven a woman folds into a much larger amount of dough that soon permeates the whole loaf. It is about growing in the Kingdom that chapter 13 deals.

Let us look at this passage for truths of the Christian life, without compartmentalizing them into simplistic boxes, but rather asking to be obedient to Christ and His challenge to us in this day and age.

In verse 23 a question was placed to the Lord. Luke is vague about who asked it. "*Someone,*" the text says, said to Him, "*Lord, will those who are saved be few?*" To have asked such a question presupposed that this someone had learned a few things from the Lord's teachings. Perhaps he or she had heard from the Lord's lips that the "*way was straight and narrow*" and hence difficult to follow. Maybe this someone recalled a teaching that emphasized that all who call upon the Master, saying "*Lord, Lord,*" do not thereby necessarily enter the Kingdom. But putting the question precisely in this way indicates perhaps a measure of mean-spiritedness, a kind of perverse joy in the fact that those who are to be saved are an exclusive few. That may be the case in fact; only God knows. But the Christlike heart will hardly rejoice and revel in the knowledge that few are saved, because that can only mean that the many will be condemned.

However, Jesus deflected the question and its hidden motives, as He so often did in His dialogues with those who questioned Him. His answer implies that He had perceived that this questioner was pretty sure he was one of the few destined for salvation. Even if the questioner was one of the "few", the Master's response shows that no one may rest in this knowledge. Of course, as far as salvation is concerned, it is not of our doing in the first instance, and it is not of our doing, alone, anywhere in the process. Salvation is given to humanity by God through Jesus Christ in the Holy Spirit, as a grace, a *charis* (literally, in Greek, *a gift*), an undeserved overspilling of divine forgiveness, love, sanctification, and transformation. But paradoxically, the Master indicates that we who respond to the gift of salvation are also responsible for making it real and actual in our lives.

"*Strive,*" He said, "*to enter by the narrow door; for many, I tell you, will seek to enter and will not be able.*" The Greek word translated *will seek* is *zetesousin*: Other similar meanings are: to ask, to beg, to petition for something. Jesus was saying that there are many people who would like very much to be saved and to have the Lord hand over salvation to them on a platter. They are willing to do things that are not too demanding or costly, not too disturbing of the normal course of their lives. Jesus knows such people very well. Jesus knows them all too well.

The Shut Door

Abruptly, Jesus entered into the story of the householder who shuts the door. When the people to whom Jesus was speaking knocked on the door asking "*Lord, open to us!*", the answer is shocking. "*I do not know where you come from!*" This answer surprised them. They began to defend themselves, and their words of defense are instructive and quite revealing.

Their first defense was this: "*We ate and drank in your presence.*" These words may merely indicate a familiarity with the

Lord. It is as if we were those people and responded: "We talk about you, we put up icons and pictures and banners and posters of you and your words in our churches and our houses. Your name is a household word for us. How can you reject us?"

But perhaps for us Orthodox Christians for whom the Eucharist is central to the life of the Church, the words are even more ominous. The Eucharist is precisely eating and drinking in the Lord's presence! Clearly it was and is a good thing for us to dwell in the Lord's house, and to sit at His table, and there to eat and drink in His presence. But Jesus' words of rejection show that, alone, this is not sufficient for the Lord to know where we are coming from.

But then comes a second line of defense. *"You taught in our streets."* The living Word of God communicated the divine message. And we are to assume that in fact these excluded people did listen, did pay attention, did seek to learn from the Teacher. Thus, their protest. They were disciples. They listened and they attended to the Master's instruction. They thought themselves to be followers of the Lord. They claimed to be His people. Yes, they had committed themselves to Him. But it is not enough!

For, you see, in His rejection of those at the door, Jesus presented two essentials for the Christian Life: the sacraments and the Word of the Lord. But He also says, that alone, these are not enough to open the doors to the Kingdom. For even though these people sit at the Lord's table and attend to His Word, they are rejected. The judgment is sharp and unambiguous- *"Depart from me!"*

What is it that makes all that precedes incapable of opening the door to the Kingdom? It is the fearsome judgment that they are *"workers of iniquity." "Depart from me,"* He cried, *"all you workers of iniquity."* To the workers of iniquity, Jesus says "You are going to Hell!" *"There you will weep and gnash your teeth, when you see Abraham and Isaac and Jacob and all the prophets in the kingdom of God and you yourselves thrust out."*

They are *workers of iniquity. Ergatai tes adikias is the Greek. Adikia* can be translated in two ways. It can be understood as lacking righteousness and as injustice. Jesus was speaking of some-thing that has to do with the actual living of life. Our deeds and our actions stand here as crucially important. They determine whether we enter into the Kingdom or not.

The Big Picture

Certainly, there is a sacramental dimension to salvation that cannot be bypassed: Baptism, Eucharist, worship, prayer, and faith all lead us to focus on the sanctifying grace of God without which there can be no salvation. Certainly, there is a personal aspect of salvation that demands from us commitment to Christ in faith for His work of salvation, growth in the knowledge of God, and a loyalty to Christ expressed by spiritually and humbly sitting at the feet of the Master and learning from Him. But Jesus' sharp words point to this other aspect as well, without which there is no salvation. "Strive," He says! "Strive to enter by the narrow door." In the context of this passage, strive means that the ethical and moral dimension of our lives is as important as our openness to God's freely given grace and our personal communion in faith with Him.

The Greek word for *strive* in this passage is *agonizesthe* which includes in its meaning the idea of determined effort and struggle. No one can struggle without a sense of responsibility on the one hand, and the consciousness of both goals and the obstacles to meeting those goals. Choice, decision-making, but most of all, doing are all implied by the Lord's command: *"Strive!"* It means that no one enters the Kingdom unless in some measure his or her life is an embodiment of righteousness and virtuous living. No wonder that in the Lord's description of the Last Judgment in chapter 25 of the Gospel of Matthew, the *only* criterion for entrance into the Kingdom is whether we have ministered to Christ as the hungry, the thirsty, the stranger, the naked, the homeless, the sick, and the prisoner!

"Did you do these things?" He asks us. It would seem that if the answer to that question is "yes," then the doors of the house of salvation will be flung open widely. But if the answer is "no,"... we will not be among the few to enter therein.

Not So Simple

Careful! Let us not rush too quickly to a conclusion! Things are not so simple. Precisely because the Lord wants to know where we are coming from, the good works can never, alone, guarantee salvation. We must sit at the Lord's table and receive His bountiful gifts with gratitude and thanksgiving (*Eucharist*). If the sacramental life means anything at all, it means recognizing that we have no life in us at all unless it comes from Him: forgiveness in Baptism; communion with the Lord in the Eucharist as members of His body; the gift of multiple graces completing and fulfilling our own weaknesses and shortcomings through the gift of the Holy Spirit and the laying on of hands and the anointing; and, all the other sacraments. Without the sacramental gift of grace there is no Christian life.

Our response to this gift of divine love begins with humbling our ego before the Giver of these gifts. It means sitting at the feet of the Master. It means a willed choice to be one of His people.

In the ancient Christian baptismal rites used in the Orthodox Church the opportunity to respond to God's gift of grace is presented to us. Before the actual Baptism takes place, the candidate (through the sponsor, in most cases) is asked a series of questions in both the present and the past tenses. "Do you reject the Devil and all of his angels, and all of his pomp...?" When the Evil One is repeatedly rejected with the words "I do reject him," the candidate is asked another question. "Do you unite yourself to Christ?" Three times it is asked, and three times the response of commitment is made, "I do unite myself to Christ!" It is then put in the past tense, with the response three times repeated, "I have united myself to Christ!" Then the candidate is instructed: "Bow down and worship Him."

Here, a second set of requirements for the Christian life is dramatically made clear. Personal commitment, the inner spiritual life, learning from the Lord in humility, and growing in personal virtue are essential if we are to enter into the life of the Kingdom.

Thirdly, as is made so clear from this passage, we need to strive to enter by the narrow door of obedience to God's will in our personal behavior and in acting on behalf of others. We must be striving to be good, upright, honest, fair, caring, virtuous people. And we must have a genuine concern for the hungry, the sick, the imprisoned, and the unjustly used as we deal with individuals and as we contribute to the struggle for justice around the world.

A Three-Sided Pyramid

These three aspects of the Christian life come together like a three-sided pyramid that includes every aspect of the Kingdom of God: sacramental life in the Church; personal relationship with God; and living righteously and working for justice. Each is essential. But each alone is inadequate. Only together, as a living and practiced reality, do they provide the numbers of the combination to unlock the door of the Kingdom.

This passage from the Gospel of Luke calls you and me to seek out what is missing from our Christian life. Our life as Christians is like a combination lock. We are to find what is missing from the combination numbers of the lock of the Christian life in our own life, and to supply it. Otherwise, the door to salvation will not open.

What is the first message here for us? Christ teaches us to grow in the living of the faith in a multi-dimensional way. Experience what it means to receive the poured-out grace of God in the sacramental life, the life of God's saving grace, without which there is no salvation. Respond in daily acts of personal commitment and humble learning at the feet of the Master. Displace your pride of heart (and mind and place and station) with the self-effacing loyalty that alone makes it possible for you to discover your true self, created and destined to become God's image and likeness. Become Godlike yourself in love for your brothers and sisters in the body of Christ, His Church, and humanity everywhere, especially for the poor, the despitefully used, the unjustly treated. Practice philanthropic love and struggle for justice wherever you can. Share the good news of the gospel of salvation, for in truth, Jesus Christ is the life of the world!

Put It All Together!

Put it all together! Let the Lord and all who would see, know by your example of worship, word, commitment, outreach, charity, struggling for justice, just where you are coming from.

Be this and do this and He will know you when you knock at the door. He will not then say to you *"I do not know where you come from."* Rather, He will say to you words of recognition and familiarity: *"Well done good and faithful servant! Enter into the joy of your master"* (Matt. 25:23).

Preliminary Reflection 2

Living in the World
The 16th Chapter of the Gospel of John

[1]*I have said all this to you to keep you from falling away.* [2]*They will put you out of the synagogues; indeed, the hour is coming when whoever kills you will think he is offering service to God.* [3]*And they will do this because they have not known the Father, nor me.*

[4]*But I have said these things to you, that when their hour comes you may remember that I told you of them. I did not say these things to you from the beginning, because I was with you.* [5]*But now I am going to him who sent me; yet none of you asks me, "Where are you going?"* [6]*But because I have said these things to you, sorrow has filled your hearts.*

[7]*Nevertheless I tell you the truth: it is to your advantage that I go away, for if I do not go away, the Counselor will not come to you; but if I go, I will send him to you.* [8]*And when he comes, he will convince the world concerning sin and righteousness and judgment:* [9]*concerning sin, because they do not believe in me;* [10]*concerning righteousness, because I go to the Father, and you will see me no more;* [11]*concerning judgment, because the ruler of this world is judged.*

¹²*I have yet many things to say to you, but you cannot bear them now.* ¹³*When the Spirit of truth comes, he will guide you into all the truth; for he will not speak on his own authority, but whatever he hears he will speak, and he will declare to you the things that are to come.* ¹⁴*He will glorify me, for he will take what is mine and declare it to you.*

¹⁵*All that the Father has is mine; therefore I said that he will take what is mine and declare it to you.* ¹⁶*"A little while, and you will see me no more; again a little while, and you will see me.*

¹⁷*Some of his disciples said to one another, "What is this that he says to us, 'A little while, and you will not see me, and again a little while, and you will see me'; and, 'because I go to the Father'?"* ¹⁸*They said, "What does he mean by 'a little while'? We do not know what he means."*

¹⁹*Jesus knew that they wanted to ask him; so he said to them, "Is this what you are asking yourselves, what I meant by saying, 'A little while, and you will not see me, and again a little while, and you will see me'?"* ²⁰*Truly, truly, I say to you, you will weep and lament, but the world will rejoice; you will be sorrowful, but your sorrow will turn into joy.* ²¹*When a woman is in travail she has sorrow, because her hour has come; but when she is delivered of the child, she no longer remembers the anguish, for joy that a child is born into the world.* ²²*So you have sorrow now, but I will see you again and your hearts will rejoice, and no one will take your joy from you.*

²³*In that day you will ask nothing of me. Truly, truly, I say to you, if you ask anything of the Father, he will give it to you in my name.* ²⁴*Hitherto you have asked nothing in my name; ask, and you will receive, that your joy may be full.* ²⁵*I have said this to you in figures; the hour is coming when I shall no longer speak to you in figures but tell you plainly of the Father.* ²⁶*In that day you will ask in my name; and I do not say to you that I shall pray the Father for you;* ²⁷*for*

the Father himself loves you, because you have loved me and have believed that I came from the Father. [28]*I came from the Father and have come into the world; again, I am leaving the world and going to the Father.*

[29]*His disciples said, "Ah, now you are speaking plainly, not in any figure!* [30]*Now we know that you know all things, and need none to question you; by this we believe that you came from God."*

[31]*Jesus answered them, "Do you now believe?* [32]*The hour is coming, indeed it has come, when you will be scattered, every man to his home, and will leave me alone; yet I am not alone, for the Father is with me.* [33]*I have said this to you, that in me you may have peace. In the world you have tribulation; but be of good cheer, I have overcome the world."*

People who are serious about being Christian often sense some conflict between the Church and the world. The values, the interests, the things that are considered important by the Church are of little concern in the world. Sometimes the world appears hostile to the Christian way of life and thinking. Orthodox Christians have learned throughout their long history to expect such things. We have known the persecutions of the Roman emperors, the domination of the Ottomans, the oppression of the commisars, the expulsions of the extremist Zionists, destruction of church buildings, and the insidious infiltration of the secularists.

Yet, at the same time we live in expectation of the Kingdom: *"Thy Kingdom come, Thy will be done on earth as it is in heaven,"* we have been taught to pray. In spite of all antagonisms, we carry with us a measured optimism with hope in the face of all apparent victories of the world. What is the source of this hope, this staying power? Some of it can be traced to the 16th Chapter of John, the subject of this reflection.

Our Unity With Christ and Each Other Faces the World

In the preceeding chapter, Jesus describes Himself as the true vine and His followers as the branches that find their life in Him (v. 5). In the sixteenth chapter, Christ speaks to us as individuals, but He quickly moves to tell us that we live the life in Christ only if we live in a spirit of love for one another. He says to us, *"This is my commandment, that you love one another"* (vv. 12-17). Our personal relationship with God and our relationship to the members of the body of Christ, the Lord's vineyard, unite us all with Christ, and through Christ, with one another.

This unity is confronted by the world. Note that the Bible uses this word in many different ways, and we understand what is meant only from the context in which it is used. The world can be God's good creation; it can be the arena into which God sent His Son; it can mean nature. But it can also mean everything that is sinfully opposed to God and His people, the Church. That is the sense in which Jesus uses the word when He turns the attention of His disciples in John 15:18-26 to the world: *"...because you are not of the world...therefore the world hates you."* The world, in this sense, is opposed and antagostic to Christ. It inevitably follows that the world will be opposed and antagonistic to us, His followers. It is a serious warning and sets the stage for the message in the next chapter. Jesus is preparing His disciples for the awful events of His crucifixion. The sixteenth chapter is presented to us in the forthcoming shadow of the Cross. Yet it speaks as pertinently to you and me today as it did then. Let's walk through the highlights of Jesus' message to us.

The World and Christians Will Clash

Chapter 16 begins with a somber assurance by Christ to His followers (vv. 1-6). Precisely because they are His followers, and the world does not follow or know either Christ or God the Father, the world is going to be negative toward Christians. The world doesn't understand what it is doing; Jesus says that the world even *thinks* it is doing good: *"The hour is coming when whoever kills you will think he is offering service to God."* So misguided and confused are its values!

Why does Jesus tell His followers these things? The old proverb says "Forewarned is forearmed." That's why. *"But I have said these things to you, that when their hour comes you may remember that I told you of them,"* Jesus says.

The Holy Spirit: Strength to Face the World

In verses seven through eleven Jesus tells His disciples that it is to their advantage that He leave them through His Death, Resurrection, and Ascension. By killing Him the world shows its sinfulness, its injustice, its unrighteousness, and its domination by Satan. But the Holy Spirit will be sent to the followers of the Lord, and the first thing the Holy Spirit will do is expose the sin, injustice, and satanic nature of the evil world. The Christians will be able to discern evil when they see it. But more than that, the Holy Spirit will let them understand the truth of God more fully than ever before (vv. 12-15). Thus, Jesus promises the Church, *"When the Spirit of truth comes, he will guide you into all the truth."*

Christians Face Trials and Difficulty

As He speaks to His disciples, Jesus tells them that just as He was abandoned, abused, ridiculed, beaten, and crucified on the Cross, they too will face difficult times when it will even appear that they are alone in the struggle against their enemies and that they are abandoned by Him (vv. 16-17). These will be times of testing: *"Truly, truly, I say to you, you will weep and lament, but the world will rejoice."* However, that suffering is not the end, it is a prelude. Through perseverance they will receive His promise: *"your sorrow will turn to joy"* (v. 20). Just as a woman finds joy in her child following the pains of labor, in the same manner, Christians will achieve fulfillment when their trials are over: *"So you have sorrow now, but I will see you again and your hearts will rejoice, and no one will take your joy from you."* It is a promise of fulfillment because the Lord will reward those who persevere.

He then says, *"Hitherto you have asked nothing in my name; ask, and you will receive, that your joy may be full"* (v. 24). Christ offers His disciples an honest and realistic hope. He doesn't say that being a Christian will mean a life without difficulty, opposition, or even hatred from the world. What He does say is that those who stick with God through the difficult times, who bear the on-slaughts of the world with the help and presence of the Holy Spirit, will ultimately find fulfillment and joy.

Christ Guarantees Victory Over the World's Evil

In the last section of chapter 16 Jesus clearly applies His words to His own saving mission and to the Death, Resurrection, and Ascension that conclude His saving mission on this earth. Jesus says He will leave the disciples and the disciples will be scattered by the Lord's enemies, thus realizing what He has been talking about (vv. 25-32).

Yet, in spite of the sureness of the coming trials and the world's hatred, Jesus gives His disciples a profound word of hope and encouragement. It is a word that fills their hearts and ours with the courage to remain true, to continue the struggle, and to work and pray in supreme confidence that the people of God and the Lord's Church can never be defeated.

Put yourself in the place of the disciples who heard these words two thousand years ago. Then, take these words into your own heart. Alone we may be weak and incapable of resisting the world and all of its wiles and forces. But we are not alone! Chapter 16 ends with words of enduring inspiration for every age and every generation of Christian (v. 33). Contemplate them: *"I have said this to you, that in me you may have peace. In the world you have tribulation; but be of good cheer, I have overcome the world!"*

Preliminary Reflection 3

Communing With The Source of Life
Three Biblical Passages

John 6:53-58

[53]*"Truly, truly, I say to you, unless you eat the flesh of the Son of man and drink his blood, you have no life in you;* [54]*he who eats my flesh and drinks my blood has eternal life, and I will raise him up at the last day.* [55]*For my flesh is food indeed, and my blood is drink indeed.* [56]*He who eats my flesh and drinks my blood abides in me, and I in him.* [57]*As the living Father sent me, and I live because of the Father, so he who eats me will live because of me.* [58]*This is the bread which came down from heaven . . . he who eats this bread will live for ever."*

Matthew 26:28

"Drink of it all of you; for this is my blood of the covenant, which is poured out for many for the forgiveness of sins."

1 Corinthians 11:26

> *"For as often as you eat this bread and drink the*
> *cup, you proclaim the Lord's death until he comes."*

You may be one of those Orthodox Christians who finds it hard to accept that frequent Holy Communion is Orthodox teaching. You learned at your mother's knee that a long and strict fast was required, so you and your family members only received Holy Communion three or four times a year. You regularly attended the Divine Liturgy (also described as the Eucharist, from the Greek word *Eucharistia*) without receiving Holy Communion.

This practice of infrequent reception of the Eucharist is not correct as far as the teaching of the Church is concerned. It developed late in our Church's history. The truth of the matter can be found in the Bible and the Holy Tradition of our Church. In this reflection, let's look at some Bible passages about Holy Communion and examine the Orthodox tradition in order to better understand the authentic teaching of the Orthodox Church concerning frequent Holy Communion.

Communion and Being A Christian

In the Bible we find at least three important verses that speak to us about the importance of Holy Communion for our Christian life. The first comes from our Lord Jesus Christ as recorded in the Gospel of John. *"Truly, truly, I say to you, unless you eat the flesh of the Son of man and drink his blood, you have no life in you; he who eats my flesh and drinks my blood has eternal life, and I will raise him up at the last day. For my flesh is food indeed and my blood is drink indeed. He who eats my flesh and drinks my blood abides in me and I in him"* (John 6:53-56).

In the Orthodox understanding, these words show us how important it is for our Christian life to receive Holy Communion. Jesus connects the reception of Holy Communion with three vital elements of Christian life:

* the living practice of our Faith *("unless you eat. . .you have no life in you"*

* our eternal destiny because *"This is the bread which came down from heaven. . .he who eats this bread will live for ever"* (Jn. 6:58).
* a promise regarding the quality of our Christian life. *He who eats. . .abides in me and I in him."*

In the understanding of the Orthodox Christian tradition, this means that being a Christian requires that we receive Holy Communion on a regular basis — frequently.

Keeping Us United With Christ

As described in the Gospel of Matthew, Jesus gave another reason at the last supper for receiving Holy Communion: *"Drink of it all of you; for this is my blood of the covenant, which is poured out for many for the forgiveness of sins"* (Mat. 26:28).

Jesus invites all of His followers and disciples to partake of Holy Communion, *"for the forgiveness of sins."* Clearly, since none of us is free from sins on a daily basis, even if our sins are not so serious as to break off our relationship with Christ and His Church, we need regular forgiveness. The argument is this: "if we sin regularly and frequently, we need forgiveness regularly and frequently."

The most important consequence of sin is that it separates us from God. Holy Communion is precisely communion with God through consuming the Body and Blood of Christ. Holy Communion brings us into union with Christ.

We need to receive Holy Communion regularly to *maintain* our union with Christ. It doesn't make sense to be a Christian and not want to be in union with Christ. Frequent reception of the Sacrament helps make that union possible.

Communion and Proclaiming The Faith

The third passage from the Bible is from St. Paul's first letter to the Christians in the city of Corinth. *"As often as you eat this bread and drink the cup, you proclaim the Lord's death until he comes"* (1 Cor. 11:26). We conduct the Divine Liturgy every

Sunday and on feast days as a witness to our faith in God and especially in His Son who came into the world for our salvation. In each Divine Liturgy we proclaim and affirm the great truth that Jesus Christ died and was resurrected to give humanity new life in the Kingdom of God.

The Kingdom of God is not only proclaimed by words; it is not only proclaimed by the "service" we conduct or the sermon we preach and hear. In fact, these elements of worship are not even mentioned here. This passage tells us that it is our participation in Holy Communion that proclaims to all who would hear that Jesus Christ is the world's Savior.

Eating the bread and drinking the cup makes the proclamation! Do you see what that means? The more frequently you receive Holy Communion with heartfelt gratitude *(eucharistia)* to God for His great gift of salvation, the more faithful you are to this commandment of the Bible. You personally, together with the entire worshipping Church, proclaim the Lord's death and His resurrection each time you receive Holy Communion. Do you also see the other side of the picture? Each time you do not receive Holy Communion when you attend the Divine Liturgy, you leave the death and resurrection of Jesus Christ *unproclaimed!*

Right and Wrong Traditions

For these reasons, the Tradition of the Church encourages frequent Holy Communion at the Divine Liturgy. We have on record the practice of early Christians receiving Holy Communion on an almost daily basis. A well-known Roman Catholic scholar of the Eastern Liturgical tradition, Fr. Robert Taft, summarizes in one of his books that "Eucharistic frequency has varied, but in the earliest of times daily communion seems to have been the ideal, and daily mass (Divine Liturgy) was known in some churches as early as the fourth century. Hence to look on such frequency as 'medieval,' or 'recent,' or 'Western,' is simply false. . . . As for the question of frequency . . . for *communion* the older norm is daily availability." In the tradition of the Church there was variety, but frequent reception of Holy Communion was the rule and infrequent reception of Holy Communion, for the greater part of the Church's history, was the exception to this rule.

For example, if you read the fourth century canons (Church rules) that have come down to us under the title *The Apostolic Canons*, you will find a very strict rule that condemns everyone who comes to the Divine Liturgy and does *not* receive Holy Communion! Canon nine reads, "All the faithful who come in and hear the Scriptures, but do not stay for the prayers and the Holy Communion, are to be excommunicated, as causing disorder in the Church." The eighth canon makes a similar requirement of the clergy.

In a small booklet published by the Greek Archdiocese of North and South America in 1942 titled *The Sacrament of Holy Communion* written by Archbishop Ierotheos Metropoulos of Patras, we are given a summary of the attitude of the Church Fathers.

In addition to the Church canons, many of the God-bearing Fathers argue, especially in their sermons, for frequent Communion, teaching this as a duty and pointing out the great benefits which come from it: the holy Justin Martyr, St. Ambrose, St. Basil, the divine Chrysostom in many of his homilies, Gregory of Thessalonica, Symeon of Thessalonica and many others. Above all, St. Chrysostom, that golden-mouthed teacher, preaches so frequently on the topic, that it is impossible for Christians to remain unconvinced that they should receive Holy Communion, both worthily and frequently.

The "traditions of men"

It can be truly strange to hear just the opposite expressed as the true position of the Orthodox Church! We refer to the Holy Tradition of the Church as its authentic voice and understanding of Divine Revelation. This might be described as "Big T" Tradition.

We can also talk, however, of "minuscule 't' traditions." Here we are talking about all kinds of practices not in harmony with the revelation communicated to us by Holy Tradition and are sometimes in direct conflict with it. The New Testament calls these practices "the tradition of men" (Col. 2:8).

Unfortunately, superstitious and simply wrong-headed practices have sometimes taken on great authority in our parish life and have been treated as if they are part of authentic Holy Tradition. Let me tell you what I believe to be the most serious example of this wrong-headed minuscule 't' tradition: the idea that somehow it is more reverent, pious, and Christian, to receive Holy Communion infrequently, than to receive Holy Communion on a frequent and regular basis! This idea is contrary to the entire Christian tradition. We need to eject minuscule 't' from our Church life, especially when it denies frequent Holy Communion.

Receiving Holy Communion Worthily

Naturally, if we receive Holy Communion frequently we should receive it "worthily." To receive worthily requires that:

* we receive with faith in Jesus Christ
* our lives express a commitment to Christ
* we have not committed major sins considered by the practice and tradition of the Church to be obstacles to our communion with Christ. If we have committed such sins, we have repented, confessed, and received forgiveness for them in the Sacrament of Holy Confession.

Receiving worthily cannot mean we are absolutely perfect when approaching the Chalice, since Holy Communion is precisely "for the forgiveness of sins." The sins we commit daily are the shortcomings and failures to live up to our potential as followers of Christ. Holy Communion is designed to help us in our struggle to follow Christ.

We can receive worthily through proper preparation. In the practice of the Church, we come to the chalice worthily through a series of practices that are designed to prepare our hearts, minds, and bodies and heal our relationships with others so that we receive Christ properly.

Perhaps, in a paradoxical way, receiving worthily means precisely that we know we are always unworthy of this great gift of God to us! One of the prayers before Holy Communion begins with the words "None is worthy" to receive Holy Communion. A legitimate concern about receiving Holy Communion frequently is that it will become a routine habit, and we will lose the sense of the awesomeness of what we are doing — we are receiving within us the Incarnate Son of God! Though this is a legitimate fear, we can guard against genuinely unworthy reception of the Sacrament by making a concerted effort to prepare our hearts, minds, feelings, and bodies to become hospitable places for Christ to enter.

The few rules we have for preparing to receive Holy Communion worthily address the physical, emotional, and spiritual aspects of our lives:

* we do not eat before coming to Holy Communion
* we abstain from sexual relations the night before
* we try to keep our emotions quiet and calm in preparation for receiving Christ's Body and Blood within us
* we seek to strengthen our relationship with Christ in advance of Holy Communion by praying more intensely
* we seek to heal our relationships with other people

These practices do not make us worthy in some absolute sense. Rather, they make us worthy by creating in us a sense of the greatness of God's love for us in our unworthiness, when He graciously offers Himself to us! If we have sinned so seriously that our whole relationship with God is in jeopardy, then we must also confess our sins to our Father Confessor before approaching the chalice for Holy Communion.

Are You Prepared?

In general, we need to look inwardly to examine our hearts to see if we are properly prepared. For example, attitudes of sustained hatred for others and persistent vices need to be in the process of continual spiritual attention. What matters is not so much that these attitudes exist, but whether we are spiritually struggling with them. When we sincerely struggle with our sinful attitudes Holy Communion helps to strengthen us in our spiritual battle. The critical question is where are our hearts?

St. Paul once addressed a situation of worthy or unworthy participation in the Eucharist. Some of the Christians in Corinth were fighting among themselves. They were rowdy, stuffed themselves with food, and drank too much wine; then they approached the chalice to receive Holy Communion! St. Paul saw that this was not the proper way to approach the Holy Chalice. Thus he responded: *"Whoever, therefore, eats the bread or drinks the cup in an unworthy manner will be guilty of profaning the body and blood of Christ"* (1 Cor. 11:27). Clearly, behavior like that exhibited by the Corinthians cannot properly prepare one's spirit to receive the Body and Blood of Christ. It *profanes* the Communion. St. Paul continues: *"Anyone who eats and drinks without discerning the body eats and drinks judgment upon himself"* (1 Cor. 11:29). Clearly, this passage requires us to receive Holy Communion with a clear consciousness of what we are doing and in a spirit of reverence.

Thus, worthy reception of the Eucharist boils down to a question of conscience, not rules. For example, a young high school graduate once went to her prom on Saturday night and got home after midnight. She went to Church the next morning and received Holy Communion. Her grandmother asked her whether this was a right thing to do.

Is dancing at a graduation dance wrong in itself? Not likely. Can it be an occasion for temptation and sinful thoughts and behaviors? Not unlikely. Is a dance a genuinely positive way to prepare a person to discern the body of the Lord? Highly unlikely.

The key is whether we approach the chalice with an attitude that properly prepares our souls to receive the Lord. Our conscience must judge it. But our conscience also needs to be informed, cultivated, and sensitive to the fact that we are preparing to receive the Son of God.

This reflection has championed frequent Holy Communion. But it must be admitted that the grandmother in this story makes an important point. When we plan to receive Holy Communion, we must reflect on what we are doing. Some quiet time, examination of conscience, prayer, and confession of sins are in order. We must learn to be discerning on a more spiritual level so that we may receive our Lord's Body and Blood as worthily as we can.

The bottom line is this. Each one of us who formally has the right to receive the Sacrament must make the decision. But the decision must be made with spiritually based criteria and in full consciousness of what we are doing. Is our soul a fit dwelling for Christ to enter? The grandmother mentioned above has encouraged us to be more careful and serious about our frequent Holy Communion.

Conclusion: Frequent Worthy Communion Needed

So you see, the Bible teaches us that Holy Communion is an essential aspect of our Christian life, both for the present and for eternity. Holy Tradition also teaches us that we need to receive Holy Communion on a frequent and regular basis because we need forgiveness to be in union with Christ. Further, it is our responsibility to let others know where we stand in our faith by "proclaiming the death and resurrection of Jesus Christ" through frequent Holy Communion. Part of that responsibility includes the requirement that we participate frequently and regularly in the Sacrament of Holy Communion.

Preparation, however, is what makes our participation in some sense worthy, even though we know that it is God *"who sees in secret"* the *"secrets of (our) heart"* (Mat. 6:4; 1 Cor. 14:25). Frequent Holy Communion cannot be understood without a clear and conscientious preparation for Holy Communion: the fast on the day we receive, prayers of preparation, an introspective heart, restoration of damaged relationships with God and others, and a grateful heart that seeks real and living communion with Christ. Do you remember the words of invitation just before the offering of the Chalice to the people in the Divine Liturgy?

With (reverent and awe-filled) fear of God, faith, and love, draw near!

The First Epistle

Is Any Among You Sick?
James 5:14-16

> ^{14}*Is any among you sick? Let him call for the elders of the church, and let them pray over him, annointing him with oil in the name of the Lord; and the prayer of faith will save the sick man, and the Lord will raise him up;* ^{15}*and if he has committed sins, he will be forgiven.* ^{16}*Therefore confess your sins to one another, and pray for one another, that you may be healed. The prayer of a righteous man has great power in its effects.*

What a question for the Bible to address to us! *"Is any among you sick?"* asks James in his letter. Throughout history, the answer to this question has been and continues to be "Yes!"

Who among us has not experienced sickness at one time or another? Some of us are chronically ill. We've all felt the debilitating influence of illness on our bodies, our minds, and even in our souls. So, the apostle James' question is in some way directed to every one of us, in the depths of our most painful personal experience. The way he proceeds to respond to that "Yes" is quite important to us. This response provides us with insights about health and illness to which we may never have previously given much thought.

The passage above should be familiar to most practicing Orthodox Christians. It is read during the Sacrament of "Prayer-

Oil" which is also known as Holy Unction. In some jurisdictions of the Orthodox Church this Sacrament is conducted only privately, while in others it is offered to individuals privately as needed, and publicly every Holy Wednesday.

A Sacrament for the Sick

Verse 14 has been understood in the Church from the very earliest times to be the scriptural basis for the establishment of the Sacrament of Holy Unction. Written documents from as early as the second century refer to the blessing of oil by the bishop, and its administration to the sick.

The Greek word *presbyterous* when translated into the English version as *elders*, can be misunderstood. It does not refer to all the older members of the congregation. Rather *presbyterous* refers to the priests of the Church. The official name given to the priest is *Presbyter*, even in English. (For more examples of this use of the word, see 1 Tim. 5:17 and Tit. 1:5.) Oil, a common ancient method of healing, is exemplified in the story Jesus told about the Good Samaritan who bound up the wounds of the man who had been robbed and beaten *"pouring on oil and wine"* (Lk. 10:34).

Here we are clearly dealing not with ordinary medicine but with a spiritual and religious act. Why? Because the anointing takes place *"in the name of the Lord"* with prayer and confidence that it is God who will heal the sick person. Though Christians respect and honor physicians and the practice of medicine and have recourse to it, they know that it is God who in fact heals our ills. The physician is important in aiding the process of healing, but it is God who is *The Healer*. This attitude was expressed a long time before St. James wrote this passage. In the Old Testament deuterocanonical book of Ecclesiasticus (also known as *Sophia Seirach*) we read these still applicable words:

> My son, in thy sickness be not negligent: but pray
> to the Lord, and he will make thee whole. Leave off
> from sin, and order thy hand aright, and cleanse thy
> heart from all wickedness. Give a sweet savour, and
> a memorial of fine flour; and make a fat offering, as
> not being. Then give place to the physician, for the

Lord hath created him: let him not go from thee, for thou hast need of him. There is a time when in their hands there is good success. For they shall also pray unto the Lord, that he would prosper that which they give for ease and remedy to prolong life (38:9-14).

The Spiritual and the Physical Together

The passages from James and Ecclesiasticus lead us to an understanding of illness which our age has just rediscovered. We have known for centuries of germs and viruses that cause illness regardless of the state of our character. For a long time, we forgot the messages of Ecclesiasticus and James; that is, the condition of our health, both physical and spiritual, is also influenced by the intangible dimensions of our lives that concern the soul. Science now recognizes psychosomatic illness (that is, soul-body ills) and strives for wholistic medicine, which treats the total person: body, emotions, mind, and spirit. That is why *the prayer of faith* is important for healing to take place. An essential aspect of healing, if it is to be complete, is for all that is disharmonious between us in our sickness, God, our fellow human beings, and nature to be put aright. Therefore, *"...if he has committed sins, he will be forgiven."*

This reconciliation is important because it is conditional. James is not saying that every sin you commit will give you some specific illness. However, there are some situations where this could be true. For example, drug or alcohol abuse is the source of some specific physical illnesses. A case in point might be the development of cirrhosis of the liver by overindulgence in alcohol.

In the main, however, James is saying that in a broad and general way our sinfulness contributes to the spiritual and physical disharmony in our bodies and the disordered state of our health. This disharmony is what the physician refers to when he speaks of psychosomatic illness.

Health in Community

James leads us further on to another important truth, going beyond Ecclesiasticus: our health and our sickness is not just a private thing. Health and sickness are part of a social whole. We sin against one another; we harm the lives of others; and, others harm our health and well-being. James says there are two things we need to do. First, we all need to continually clear the air from the moral and spiritual pollution of our unkindnesses and our unloving behavior to one another: *"Therefore,"* he says in verse 16, *"confess your sins to one another."*

This confession of sins is the necessary and essential prelude to mutual forgiveness and the restoration of peace in the body of the Church and the body of society. But confession alone is not enough if true health is to come to us, in us, and among us. Secondly, James tells us we must take an active interest in the welfare of one another for healing to come in its fullness: *"pray for one another, that you might be healed."* This concern is not restricted to the physically sick alone. Prayer for the sick is spiritual therapy, for sure. But prayer for those who are healthy is a kind of preventive medicine designed to keep us in harmony with God, our neighbor, and yes, with ourselves.

The Prayer of a Righteous Man

James points to an even greater source of healing for us as he concludes this teaching. *"The prayer of a righteous man has great power in its effects."* Since its beginning, the Church has taken those words to heart and has called upon those special people who lived so close to our Lord that they were His friends.

The friends of God are the saints. We certainly can pray for healing directly to God, and we should. We certainly can ask our fellow believers to pray for us, just as James tells us. With just as much certainty we have the confidence that we can ask the blessed saints to pray for us in our need, for *"the prayer of a righteous man has great power in its effects."* Perhaps that is why the Church routinely seeks the intercessions of the saints for all purposes, including the healing of sickness.

What To Do?

"Is any among you sick?" The response James gives us to that question challenges us to respond to the Word of God by:

* accepting the healing grace of the Sacrament of Holy Unction
* availing ourselves of the ministrations of the medical arts
* recognizing the whole situation of healthiness and un-healthiness
* giving and receiving forgiveness as a way of clearing away the sinful and disharmonious caring for others through prayer
* availing ourselves of the great power of God's saints for healing

Jesus once asked a man who had been ill for thirty-eight years and who lay unable to do anything for himself at the pool of Bethesda: "Do you want to be healed?" (Jn. 5:5). He asks the same question to each of us today, as well. The paralyzed man responded that he had no one to help him reach the healing waters of the pool. We can't say that. For we have the words of James 5:14-16.

The First Gospel

Justifying Ourselves
Luke 10:25-37

^{25}And behold, a lawyer stood up to put him to the test, saying, "Teacher, what shall I do to inherit eternal life?" ^{26}He said to him, "What is written in the law? How do you read?" ^{27}And he answered, "You shall love the Lord your God with all your heart, and with all your soul, and with all your strength, and with all your mind; and your neighbor as yourself." ^{28}And he said to him, "You have answered right; do this, and you will live."

^{29}But he, desiring to justify himself, said to Jesus, "And who is my neighbor?" ^{30}Jesus replied, "A man was going down from Jerusalem to Jericho, and he fell among robbers, who stripped him and beat him, and departed, leaving him half dead. ^{31}Now by chance a priest was going down that road; and when he saw him he passed by on the other side. ^{32}So likewise a Levite, when he came to the place and saw him, passed by on the other side. ^{33}But a Samaritan, as he journeyed, came to where he was; and when he saw him, he had compassion, ^{34}and went to him and bound up his wounds, pouring on oil and wine; then he set him on his own beast and brought him to an inn, and took care of him. ^{35}And the next day he took out two denarii and gave them to the innkeeper, saying, 'Take care of

> *him; and whatever more you spend, I will repay you when I come back.' *[36]*Which of these three, do you think, proved neighbor to the man who fell among the robbers?"* [37]*He said, "The one who showed mercy on him." And Jesus said to him, "Go and do likewise."*

Sometimes the truth bothers us, especially when we are wrong. Even if we accept the truth with our mind and we know in our heart that someone is telling us the real truth about ourselves, it is so hard, so costly, to accept the truth when we are wrong.

Getting Caught By The Truth

When one of the smart, well-placed, good-hearted, professional, lawyers of Jewish religious affairs asked Jesus what he needed to do *to inherit eternal life*, Jesus asked him in response to describe what was written in the Old Testament law. The lawyer knew what he had to say. He answered his own question: to gain eternal life he should love God completely and love his neighbor the same way. When the Lord said, *"You have answered right; do this, and you will live,"* he knew he had been caught! He felt it.

Accepting The Truth

Jesus told the lawyer what he already knew about himself. Then why did the lawyer ask? The passage tells us his motive: *"to put him (Jesus) to the test."* The Greek verb is *peirazo* and it carries the connotation of tempting or trapping someone.

The lawyer was trying to make Jesus look bad. Without any sense of retribution, Jesus' answer puts the lawyer on the spot. It was as if Jesus told him, "If you knew the answer all the time, then, instead of asking me, you should be loving God and your neighbor, not talking about it." It was a classic case of someone being told a hard-to-accept truth. You don't need much imagination to step into the lawyer's shoes and feel what he felt. Jesus knows our hearts and His word uncovers all of our pretenses. But often, rather than accept the truth about ourselves we try to escape, even when the words have struck home.

Justifying Ourselves

Well, that's how it was with the lawyer. For us, the dialogue between Jesus and the lawyer is a blessing because it became the occasion for Jesus to tell the story of the Good Samaritan. For you see, when the lawyer saw that he had been put on the spot, the Bible tells us he acted in a predictable way: *"But he, desiring to justify himself, said to Jesus, 'And who is my neighbor?'"*

Jesus' answer to that question was the parable of the Good Samaritan. Let us look at the phrase *"desiring to justify himself"* which in Greek is *dikaioun.* One well-known commentator translates this word as wishing to put himself in the right, pointing to the human unwillingness to hear words of guidance and correction because they threaten our ego. Our immediate response is to defend our threatened ego when words of correction become uncomfortable.

Jesus allows the lawyer to shift the weight of the accusation so that He can tell the story. At the end of the parable, Jesus presses the same conclusion on the lawyer: *"Which of these three (the priest, the levite, the Samaritan), do you think, proved neighbor to the man who fell among the robbers?" He said, "The one who showed mercy on him." And Jesus said to him, "Go and do likewise."* It is the very same injunction Jesus gave to the lawyer before He told the parable.

Personal Lessons

There is a very personal lesson in this parable. It is precisely when we are put on the spot by our conscience that we have to be very careful about how we respond. Our almost instinctive reaction is to do what the lawyer did: to get defensive and to try to justify ourselves. If we're listening to the Lord however, that just won't do. This passage teaches us that when we are told the truth about ourselves a defensive and justifying posture is precisely *not* the appropriate response.

However, neither should we wallow in guilt. Jesus never accused or condemned the lawyer though he was certainly guilty. that's for sure. Emphasizing his guilt is not Jesus' intention. Rather, Jesus wants the man to change. He doesn't want to put him down. He doesn't want to shame him. He doesn't want him to put up a shield of defense for his wounded pride. What *does* Jesus want of the lawyer, and of you and me? He wants us to change, to act, to *do* what is right.

What To Do?

> *You have answered right; do this, and you will live."*
>
> *And Jesus said to him, "Go and do likewise."*

Jesus is telling the lawyer and us that life's moments of vulnerability are great opportunities for growth. When someone speaks the truth about us in a way that exposes us, it is a critical spiritual occasion. If we react by protecting our bruised egos, we lose a precious opportunity to change, to go beyond our present spiritual level, to act in a new way that makes us come into closer harmony with God's will. In short, we lose the opportunity to become more Godlike human beings.

You know the experience. Next time it comes, let it be a challenge to you to grow, to really grow. Don't close up the battle lines. Acknowledge the truth about yourself and do something about it.

Oh yes! Do you know what the Church calls this process? There is a special word for it: Repentance.

The Second Epistle

Maintaining Unity Among Christians
Romans 15:1-6

> ¹*We who are strong ought to bear with the failings of the weak, and not to please ourselves;* ²*let each of us please his neighbor for his good, to edify him.* ³*For Christ did not please himself; but, as it is written, "The reproaches of those who reproached thee fell on me."* ⁴*For whatever was written in former days was written for our instruction, that by steadfastness and by the encouragement of the scriptures we might have hope.* ⁵*May the God of steadfastness and encouragement grant you to live in such harmony with one another, in accord with Christ Jesus,* ⁶*that together you may with one voice glorify the God and Father of our Lord Jesus Christ.*

One of the important things about the Christian life we need to understand is that every member is at a different level of Christian growth. The Orthodox Christian faith teaches us that we are called to grow as Christians in the image and the likeness of God. That's part of what we mean when we say that the goal of Christians is to achieve Godlikeness, or, to use the more theological word, *Theosis*.

The fact that we are all at different levels of growth means that there are many occasions when we will not always see things in the same way. Nor will we act the same way in similar circumstances. That can create trouble among us. I'm sure that you can think of such situations in your parish. I know that there have been plenty of them in mine! The Bible shows us that such problems existed even in the early, Apostolic Church. The subject of this reflection on the Word of God is how to handle ourselves when there are differences of understanding about how to think and act, especially when we are a little advanced in our Christian understanding and growth.

Early Problems Among Christians

In chapter 14 of his letter to the Romans, St. Paul deals with some questions that were creating conflicts among the believers in Rome: whether Christians should eat meat, or be vegetarians; whether Christians were permitted to drink wine, observe holidays, and so forth. There Paul responds by appealing for mutual understanding and forbearance. So, he asks in verse 10 *"Why do you pass judgment on your brother? Or you, why do you despise your brother?"* And, toward the end of chapter 14, he says that we have an obligation not to create problems for our brothers and sisters in the faith: *"...it is right not to eat meat or drink wine or do anything that makes your brother stumble"* (vv. 21).

From the Negative to the Positive

In chapter 15, St. Paul moves from telling us that we should not do anything that will be detrimental to our fellow Christians, to something more positive. *"We who are strong ought to bear with the failings of the weak, and not to please ourselves; let each of us please his neighbor for his good, to edify him"* (v. 1-2).

When we see a fellow Christian whose thinking or behavior is less than ideal, we are called to try to understand where this Christian is coming from. St. Paul calls these Christians *weak*, in the Greek, *asthenemata ton adynaton.* Modern Greeks use the first word to mean sickness but it literally means without strength. The word *adynaton* refers to those without power or ability to act. St. Paul calls us to deal with these kinds of Christians from within their own frame of reference, their own limited and restricted understanding of what it means to be a Christian. We are not to be self-centered; we are not to *"please ourselves."*

St. Paul admonishes us to put ourselves in our weaker brother's or sister's shoes, see things from his or her perspective, then seek to address the problem from his or her perspective for his or her benefit, growth, and development! What a tremendous guideline for parish relations! This is what he says: *"...let each of us please his neighbor for his good, to edify him."* The Greek word for edify literally means to build a house, that is, to build up the other person in Christian understanding and life, not tear him down, criticize, or condemn him.

Why Christians Should Act This Way

Why should Christians act this way toward their fellow Christians, even when they don't act properly or when they create problems? St. Paul tells us why in verses 3 and 4. The answer is straightforward and it not only tells us why we should do it, but also how we can keep learning how to do it, and how to keep getting inspiration on how to do it. *"For Christ did not please himself..."*, he says. Christ himself is our example. Why? Precisely because we are called to be like God, and Jesus shows us precisely what that means!

St. Paul quotes a passage from the first translation of the Hebrew scriptures, the Septuagint, Psalm 68:10 (RSV 69:9). The twelfth century Orthodox biblical commentator, Zigabenos understands this passage to mean the following: "Having set as His goal *our* salvation, Jesus put aside his own glory and having been crucified, he appeared powerless and was reproached, as is written in the book of the Psalms." So Jesus himself bore the *"failings of the weak,"* and *"did not please himself,"* but rather acted for our good, to edify us. Paul then proceeds to tell us that the Bible offers us *"instruction"* and *"encouragement"* as we seek to follow the example of Jesus Christ.

Living and Worshiping Together

St. Paul knows we are all different and that differences will always exist among us. Nevertheless, he sets up a goal and a pattern by which we need to always measure our lives as parishioners, and he shows us the major means for achieving the goal: *"May the God of steadfastness and encouragement grant you to live in such harmony with one another, in accord with Christ Jesus, that together you may with one voice glorify the God and Father of our Lord Jesus Christ"* (vv. 5-6).

He wants us to act, but he knows that God's grace will bring about *"harmony with one another."* The goal of this harmony is to glorify, praise, honor, and confess our God in shared worship with one voice. We're reminded of the words of the Divine Liturgy: "Let us love one another, that with one accord we may confess Father, Son, and Holy Spirit, the Trinity, one in essence and undivided."

The First Step in Dealing With Parish Controversies

There it is, a straightforward prescription for parish unity. Next time someone creates a problem in your parish, you now know what to do. Before you do anything else, reread Romans 15:1-6.

The Second Gospel

What Happens When a Sinner Meets Christ?
Luke 19:1-10

> [1]He entered Jericho and was passing through. [2]And there was a man named Zacchaeus; he was a chief tax collector, and rich.
>
> [3]And he sought to see who Jesus was, but could not, on account of the crowd, because he was small of stature. [4]So he ran on ahead and climbed up into a sycamore tree to see him, for he was to pass that way. [5]And when Jesus came to the place, he looked up and said to him, "Zacchaeus, make haste and come down; for I must stay at your house today."
>
> [6]So he made haste and came down, and received him joyfully. [7]And when they saw it they all murmured, "He has gone in to be the guest of a man who is a sinner."
>
> [8]And Zacchaeus stood and said to the Lord, "Behold, Lord, the half of my goods I give to the poor; and if I have defrauded any one of anything, I restore it fourfold."
>
> [9]And Jesus said to him, "Today salvation has come to this house, since he also is a son of Abraham. [10]For the Son of man came to seek and to save the lost."

What happens when a sinner meets Christ? We learn the answer to this question in the story of the short chief tax collector of Jericho. Most of us know that Zacchaeus wanted to see Jesus when He travelled through the town but wasn't able to because the taller people got in front of him. So he ran ahead, climbed a tree, and got a look. We also know that Jesus saw him, called him, entered his house for a meal, and called him saved when he offered to make restitution for his wrongdoings. In this reflection we are going to look at this story a bit more carefully.

An Unquestioned Sinner

No one in Jericho questioned that Zacchaeus was a sinner, except Zacchaeus. Verse 2 reveals this truth about Zacchaeus in a cryptic manner for us, but very clearly for any first-century Jew: *"he was a chief tax-collector, and rich."* Zacchaeus was employed by the pagan Roman government. He was a high official of the oppressive system. He was clearly in a position to extort unjust taxes. Finally, he was rich; this meant to the people that in fact he did exploit them. Clearly, he was a sinner!

A Sinner Seeks Jesus

Nevertheless, something in Zacchaeus was moved to want to see Jesus when He came through town. It was more than curiosity, it would seem. Verse 3 reads: *"he sought to see who Jesus was."* That reveals a more serious interest than mere curiosity. He must have heard things about Jesus. Clearly, seeing Jesus was important enough to Zacchaeus that he made a special effort to see Him. Zacchaeus' heart was searching for something. . . . Maybe Jesus could supply it!

I suppose the crowd milled around Jesus as He walked so that finally Zacchaeus gave up trying to get close to Jesus. He then decided to *"run ahead,"* and as verse 4 tells us, he climbed up into a *"sycamore tree."* Scholars dispute just what kind of tree it was. Some say it was the type with low branches parallel to the ground, that make a kind of natural ladder. There is no hint that this rather prominent man of Jericho was embarrassed to climb up the tree. It was so important for him to see Jesus!

Jesus Seeks The Sinner

Then it happened. Just as Jesus was coming by the tree, He stopped and looked right at Zacchaeus. Jesus addressed him personally and by name: *"Zacchaeus, make haste and come down . . . ."* Zacchaeus hungered to see Jesus and Jesus responded to that hunger. Jesus knew Zacchaeus' name! He spoke directly to him! Then Jesus immediately ordered Zacchaeus to come down from the tree. This was directly related to an unbelievable and totally unexpected fulfillment of Zacchaeus' heartfelt desire to see Jesus. Verse 5 continues, *"...for I must stay at your house today."* Can you believe that? Zacchaeus made a special effort to reach out to Christ, and Christ not only saw him, but He talked to him and called him by name. And then, wonder of wonders! Christ told Zacchaeus that He intended to go into his house! When you meet Christ, all kinds of fabulous things can happen!

The Sinner Responds to the Lord

So what are you to do? The presence of God is overwhelming! Once you catch your breath you respond to the Lord. First, you immediately do what He tells you to do. *"So he made haste and came down, and received him joyfully."* Notice these words in verse 6, *"and received him joyfully."* You not only do what the Lord tells you to do, you also *receive Him.* Into your heart. Into your life. Into your thoughts. Into your entire being. That means a big change in your life, especially if everyone knows that you are a big sinner!

Judges of the Sinner

It's difficult for people to accept repentance in others, especially when they are big sinners. It is so difficult, that all those people crowding around the Lord just a few minutes before Zacchaeus came into the picture, praising and fawning over Him, suddenly had a turn of mind.

Verse 7 describes their reaction: *"...they all murmured, 'He has gone in to be the guest of a man who is a sinner.'"* Christ saw what was in Zacchaeus' heart: the hunger for communion with God; the thirst for cleansing and purification; the desire to stand justified before God and man; the need to put away the history of human disfigurement. And Jesus called Zacchaeus by name. He recognized him as a person. He told him what to do. Jesus wanted to come to be with him in his own house. But the people were blind to all that. They not only judged Zacchaeus (*"a man who is a sinner"*); they even murmured against Jesus!

The Sinner Changes

Look at what happens when a sinner meets Jesus. Standing next to Christ, Zacchaeus sees fully who he is. The people, no doubt, had frequently charged him with being a sinner. Surely, he knew they were aware of his injustices as the head tax collector. But he never repented, in spite of the fact that they condemned him and called him a sinner. That attitude never leads people to repentance.

Now, however, in the presence of the Sinless One, Zacchaeus sees and readily acknowledges his own unworthiness, like a lady placing a worn-out house dress next to a beautiful jeweled evening gown. The shabbiness of the old dress is all the more noticeable next to the luxurious gown. When Christ meets sinners, they see themselves as they are.

As a result, Zacchaeus repented of his former deeds of injustice. He admitted his sin and then acted on it: *"Behold, Lord, the half of my goods I give to the poor."* Zacchaeus responded in gratitude for what Christ had done for him, a case of genuine stewardship. But more than that happens when a sinner meets Christ. Verse 8 quotes Zacchaeus *"...and if I have defrauded any one of anything, I restore it fourfold."* Here Zacchaeus did what the Old Testament defined as just. When something was stolen or taken unjustly, justice required that it be returned by one-fifth more of its value to the rightful owner (Num. 5:6-7). When that which was taken unjustly could not be itself returned, then justice demanded a fourfold payment (Exod. 22:3, 8; 4 Kingdom 12:6 [Septuagint]). But the important thing to notice is that Zacchaeus didn't do this because he was told to, but because he had now received Christ into his life, and he began to act, think, and desire in a new and different way.

Salvation Is Given to the Sinner

Zacchaeus was a new person! A person no longer distorted by sin. A person who was once again whole. The New Testament Greek word for salvation is *soteria*. The root of this word is *soos* which means whole or complete. Salvation is wholeness that comes from a complete relationship with God, with neighbor, and with oneself. It requires the right orientation to life. To be saved is to have our humanity, as created in God's image and likeness, restored. This is one aspect of salvation, and that's what happened to Zacchaeus, the sinner.

Zacchaeus was now clear on the real values of life. Jesus put it definitively in verse 9: *"Today salvation has come to this house."* Zacchaeus was no longer spiritually and morally exiled from the people of God, whether they wanted to recognize it or not... *"since he also is a son of Abraham."* He sought out Christ, who welcomed him. He responded to Jesus' acceptance of him with acts that reflected his new relationship with God. This new relationship with God created a new relationship with his neighbors against whom he had sinned in the past. Jesus was no longer a stranger to Zacchaeus. Jesus went to Zacchaeus' home, sat down at his dining room table, and ate with Zacchaeus and his fellow tax collectors. It was a new relationship! Zacchaeus had changed! He was a new man!

"Lord, Have Mercy"

The biblical story doesn't tell us what happened after Jesus visited the home of Zacchaeus: whether the people of Jericho also sincerely received Christ, or whether they were able to accept Zacchaeus back into their community life. We can only guess at that.

In the tradition of the Church, however, Zacchaeus subsequently lived his life as a follower of Christ, a member of the Church. He is commemorated as a saint on April 20. We don't have much more information about him, but we are told in the lives of the saints that he became an apostle of our Lord, seeking to proclaim the message of Christ for others to believe and to follow the Christian way.

The story of Zacchaeus clearly teaches that when a sinner meets Christ,

* the Lord cares enough to personally respond to his or her need to find forgiveness and redemption
* ways are given for repentance
* guidance is provided for a new life
* an inner change takes place which makes life new

In ordinary Church language, when a sinner meets Christ, we speak of a change of heart and mind. We also speak of repentance, that is, turning away from our old and sinful ways of living and seeking to be in communion with God. Perhaps this is why *Kyrie Eleison* (Lord have mercy) is repeated over and over again in the Divine Lilturgy and every other service of the Church. It seems that perpetual repentance is an essential element for a Godlike life!

Do you think that Zacchaeus just might be a model for the rest of us?

The Third Epistle – Reflection 1

A More Excellent Way
1 Corinthians 12:27-13:8

²⁷*Now you are the body of Christ and individually members of it.* ²⁸*And God has appointed in the church first apostles, second prophets, third teachers, then workers of miracles, then healers, helpers, administrators, speakers in various kinds of tongues.* ²⁹*Are all apostles? Are all prophets? Are all teachers? Do all work miracles?* ³⁰*Do all possess gifts of healing? Do all speak with tongues? Do all interpret?*

³¹*But earnestly desire the higher gifts.*

And I will show you a still more excellent way.

¹*If I speak in the tongues of men and of angels, but have not love, I am a noisy gong or a clanging cymbal.* ²*And if I have prophetic powers, and understand all mysteries and all knowledge, and if I have all faith, so as to remove mountains, but have not love, I am nothing.*

³*If I give away all I have, and if I deliver my body to be burned, but have not love, I gain nothing.*

⁴*Love is patient and kind; love is not jealous or boastful;* ⁵*it is not arrogant or rude. Love does not insist on its own way; it is not irritable or resentful;* ⁶*it does not rejoice at wrong, but rejoices in the right.* ⁷*Love bears all things, believes all things, hopes all things, endures all things.* ⁸*Love never ends; as for*

> *prophecies, they will pass away; as for tongues, they will cease; as for knowledge, it will pass away.*

One of the most popular and widely read chapters of the New Testament is the "Love Chapter" in St. Paul's first letter to the Christians in the Greek city of Corinth. Only eight verses long, it begins with the words *"If I speak in the tongues of men and angels, but have not love, I am a noisy gong or a clanging cymbal."* It ends with the famous words "So faith, hope, love abide, these three; but the greatest of these is love."

Many excellent commentaries, both ancient and modern, have explained the meaning of love as it is presented to us in the thirteenth chapter of 1 Corinthians. In the two reflections that follow, we will look at the "Love Chapter" more carefully from within the patristic tradition of the Orthodox Church. But in this reflection, we will examine something about this passage that speaks to us regarding our roles as clergy, parish leaders, workers, and members.

Ins and Outs?

Notice that the five verses preceding chapter 13 talk about the various roles of the Christian believers during the period of the Apostolic Church. You'll see that verse 27 sets the stage: *"Now you are the body of Christ and individually members of it."* This passage points to a great truth that needs to be relearned by many Orthodox Christians today.

For a long time now, Orthodox have labored under the delusion that somehow, the clergy were really the in people of the Church that is, the really religious people, who were supposed to be religious and who did religious things. In contrast, the lay people were in some way on the outside. Yes, they were members of the Church, but somehow they were second-class Christians who didn't have to be so religious.

In 1 Corinthians 12:27-31, however, St. Paul destroys this myth for us. The Church, he has taught in the first part of chapter 12, is the *"body of Christ."* You see, each of us Christians is a *member* of that Body, just as your hand, or foot, or head, or eye is a member of your own physical body. *You,* in the verse refers to all of the Christians in Corinth, and by extension, to every Christian in your parish, in whatever city you live. All of us are *"individually members of"* the Church! The amazing reality is that among Orthodox Christians, there are no ins and outs. We are all members of the Body of Christ, the Church.

Each With His or Her Responsibility

Please note something important here! Being members of the Body of Christ doesn't mean that we have the same roles in the Church. Though we are all equally members of the Body of Christ (the Church), St. Paul teaches that we are not all called to the same roles and responsibilities in the Body. Previously, (1 Cor. 12:19-21), St. Paul pointed out the obvious: *"If all were a single organ, where would the body be? As it is, there are many parts, yet one body. The eye cannot say to the hand, 'I have no need of you,' nor again the head to the feet, 'I have no need of you.'"*

In verse 28 St. Paul named some of the roles: *"And God has appointed in the church first apostles, second prophets, third teachers, then workers of miracles, then healers, helpers, administrators, speakers in various kinds of tongues."* Furthermore, he emphasized that not all do everything that others do: *"Are all apostles? Are all prophets?"* and so on. What he is saying to us today is that it is important for us to realize that we all have important roles to fulfill in the Church, special callings to exercise, and significant contributions to make in our own special ways.

You, I, our neighbors, your priest, your bishop, the Sunday School teachers, the Sunday School supervisor, the parish council president, the parish council members, the singers, the members and leaders of choirs, women's groups, financial leadership groups, members of young people's organizations, other Church organizations and committees, and all parish members have been called by God to be essential members of the working Body of Christ!

Important, But Not Most Important

There seem to be two extreme responses to this truth of role and responsibility in the Church. Church members either refuse to accept the responsibilities for their role as members of the Body of Christ or they tend to make too much of their role! Thus far in this reflection, we have seen how St. Paul emphasized the need for each of us to recognize the importance of our membership in the Body of Christ and our responsibility to live up to its demands in our own special way. That's a lesson many of us Orthodox Christians have to learn and begin to put into practice!

However, it is possible that some of us, both clergy and laity, make too much of our roles. We may become self-important. We may focus upon our dignity, the respect due us, the honors, and the distinctions we feel are owed to us. Yes, we may even get to the point of demanding first places for ourselves, and looking down on the others, especially when our roles, *are*, in fact, important to the life of the Church!

It is precisely when we have these important roles that we should be careful they don't blind us to what is *really* important! As significant as our roles are, St. Paul taught that there is something more important. That is why he wrote in the last verse of chapter 12, *"I will show you a still more excellent way."*

You see, St. Paul wants to teach us that more important than our important roles, there is a *"still more excellent way."* And that is the way of love. Above all roles, positions, and offices in the Body of Christ is the need to be loving. In the next two reflections, we will ask ourselves what love *doesn't* and *does* mean.

The Third Epistle – Reflection 2

Love: What It Isn't
1 Corinthians 13:1-6

> ¹*If I speak in the tongues of men and of angels, but have not love, I am a noisy gong or a clanging cymbal.* ²*And if I have prophetic powers, and understand all mysteries and all knowledge, and if I have all faith, so as to remove mountains, but have not love, I am nothing.* ³*If I give away all I have, and if I deliver my body to be burned, but have not love, I gain nothing.* ⁴*Love is patient and kind; love is not jealous or boastful;* ⁵*it is not arrogant or rude. Love does not insist on its own way; it is not irritable or resentful;* ⁶*it does not rejoice at wrong, but rejoices in the right.*

What is love? What kind of question is that? Most of us have some idea about what love is, but isn't that the problem? There are so many ideas about what love is, that it isn't so clear to us any more. Perhaps the Bible can help us separate our mistaken ideas about love from the real meaning of love.

The thirteenth chapter of St. Paul's first letter to the Corinthian Christians is one of the all-time classical descriptions of Christian love. What is love? To answer that question St. Paul begins by letting us know that there are lots of important things in the Christian life that, in the last analysis, don't count if love is absent from them. Among these are things like eloquence (*"tongues of men and angels"*); or insight and knowledge (*"prophetic powers and understand(ing) and . . . knowledge"*); or even faith that can *"move mountains."* Even doing deeds of charity and sacrifice don't mean much if love is missing from them: *"If I give away all I have, and if I deliver my body to be burned, but have not love, I gain nothing."*

St. Paul then described some of the ways love does not behave. We will look at these in this reflection. Then in the following reflection, we will see what St. Paul wrote about what love does do.

Important Things That Don't Count

In the first verse St. Paul referred to *"speaking the tongues of men and angels."* The *"tongues of men,"* can easily be understood as the gift and talent given to some of the Corinthian Christians to instruct others about the faith. Teaching is an important role in the Church. The *"tongues of angels"* is what St. Paul called the ecstatic and emotional spiritual phenomenon by which some believers uttered understandable syllables as a way of expressing their spiritual experience of the Holy Spirit. St. Paul did not think highly of this phenomenon unless it was used to help others. Good as these gifts may be, if they are exercised without love, St. Paul wrote, the result is of no benefit to those who do them. They become senseless noise: *"a noisy gong or a clanging cymbal."*

In verse two, St. Paul turned to the role of the prophets, that is, those who *"have prophetic powers and understand all mysteries and all knowledge."* In today's Church, the role of the prophet might be that of the spiritual father or the thunderous preacher. In additon, St. Paul naturally connected prophets with those who are very knowledgeable of the teaching of the Church, those who teach the teachers. Today we would identify these people as the Church's theologians.

In this same verse, St. Paul added another group of important believers: those whose faith is very strong, that is, those who *"have all faith, so as to remove mountains."* Many of the most important people of the Church have no official position, but through their faith they influence us all in powerful ways. Then, in verse three, two other very important functions in the Church are identified:

philanthropy and martyrdom. *"If I give away all I have, and if I deliver my body to be burned, but have not love, I gain nothing."*

Pretty grim, isn't it? All these important contributions to the life of the church: teaching, prophetic inspiration, the gift of tongues, spiritual guidance, theological knowledge, profound faith, philanthropy and even martyrdom for the faith, are not at all important in the eyes of God, if they are not accompanied by one really important characteristic of the Christian life — *love!* But just what is love?

Describing the Indescribable

How does one describe love? If we don't know what it is, how can we practice it? Well, that is St. Paul's dilemma in verses four through six. In reality, we know what love is, only because we have experienced being loved. St. John said, *"In this is love, not that we loved God, but that he loved us and sent his Son"* to us for our salvation (1 Jn. 4:10). So, it is very difficult to define love, probably impossible. In the face of the reality of the difficulty of defining love, Saint Paul described some of the ways love acts and some of the behaviors love avoids. Here, love is not described for what it is in itself (God), nor is it described in terms of feelings or motives. Rather, St. Paul describes love by the way it causes us to act and by the things it does not do.

What Love Does Not Do

In this section we are presented with eight things that love does not do.

* love is not *jealous or boastful*
* love is not *arrogant or rude*
* love does *not insist on its own way*
* love is *not irritable or resentful*
* love does *not rejoice at wrong.*

If we use our imagination a little, bringing to mind specific situations when we ourselves acted in the manner described by these negatives, we can recognize one fundamental inner attitude in all of them.

What is common to all the negatives? Self-centeredness. When we are *jealous* we want for ourselves the things that others have. When we are *boastful* we are drawing attention to ourselves and away from others. When we are *arrogant* we project ourselves at the expense of others' feelings and significance. When we are *rude,* we only think of our interest and not the feelings of other people. *Insisting on your own way* is a way of telling others that they don't count and that their ideas pale in front of our views. Being *irritable* means we say things based on our own bad feelings, not considering how those sharp and hostile words affect others. *Resentment* means we nurse your hurts, coloring all our relationships with others in the light of some real or imagined past injustice we have suffered. And finally, *rejoicing at wrong* means we feel good when others fail or do wrong because it makes us look better in comparison! All the negatives point to a selfish attitude! Such an attitude can never reflect the way God deals with us. For He is not selfish.

In the traditional teaching of the Church's spiritual guides and fathers, this vice of selfishness is described as *pride.* Some even say that the sin of Adam and Eve was precisely this pride. It consisted of wanting to be like gods, by acting on their own, separate from God Himself. In recent years a well-known popular singer sang a song with the refrain "I did it my way." Not God's way! But my way! By doing "it my way" we put ourselves in the center of the universe, not only rejecting the claims of others upon us, not only ignoring the obvious dependency we have on others, not only refusing to respond to our responsibility toward others, but making ourselves and our self-interests the primary motivation of life!

Rejoicing in the Right

There is, of course, a wholesome aspect of pride. This pride identifies with the good that others do, acknowledging their lives and contributions and deriving satisfaction from their accomplishments, especially when they are godly and uplifting. Take, for example, the hymn in honor of St. Gregory the Wonderworker, whose memory is celebrated especially in Thessalonika in northern Greece:

"O Gregory the Wonderworker, light of Orthodoxy, support and teacher of the Church, glory of monks and invincible protector of theologians, *pride of Thessalonike* and preacher of grace, pray without ceasing for the salvation of our souls."

This pride is what St. Paul referred to when he wrote that love *"rejoices in the right."* We can appropriately be proud of the accomplishments of others and be humbly proud even of our own accomplishments, so long as we continuously recognize that we accomplish no good thing in life without the help and grace of God: *"Every good endowment and every perfect gift is from above, coming down from the Father of lights"* (Ja. 9:9). Naturally, being humbly proud means that we recognize the good we do not as our own doing but as coming from God, Whose instrument we become. Whatever good we do manifests God, and therefore is *His* glory, not ours!

God is Love!

The same can be said about love. Our love manifests God's love. St. John put it well when he wrote: *"We love, because he (God) first loved us"* (1 Jn. 4:19). In the same letter we read, *"He who does not love does not know God; for God is love"* (1 Jn. 4:8). God is *Love* in Himself because He is a Trinity of loving persons and because He cares about us, our welfare, and our good. This second kind of Godly love cares about others. It acts without thought of personal gain from doing good for others. That is what love does! We will see what St. Paul says about this in the next reflection. Let us first understand that when we act selfishly we are not acting in love.

The Third Epistle – Reflection 3

Love: What It Does
1 Corinthians 13:4-13

⁴*Love is patient and kind; love is not jealous or boastful;* ⁵*it is not arrogant or rude. Love does not insist on its own way; it is not irritable or resentful;* ⁶*it does not rejoice at wrong, but rejoices in the right.* ⁷*Love bears all things, believes all things, hopes all things, endures all things.*

⁸*Love never ends; as for prophecies, they will pass away; as for tongues, they will cease; as for knowledge, it will pass away.* ⁹*For our knowledge is imperfect and our prophecy is imperfect;* ¹⁰*but when the perfect comes, the imperfect will pass away.* ¹¹*When I was a child, I spoke like a child, I thought like a child, I reasoned like a child; when I became a man, I gave up childish ways.* ¹²*For now we see in a mirror dimly, but then face to face. Now I know in part; then I shall understand fully, even as I have been fully understood.*

¹³*So faith, hope, love abide, these three; but the greatest of these is love.*

How does one describe love? In the previous reflection we came to understand that St. Paul did not give us a formal definition of love in his famous "Love Chapter"; he discounted many important roles in the Church as having no value in the sight of God if they are not practiced with love; and, he indicated what love does not do, that is, love does not act selfishly. But St. Paul also teaches us what love *does* do. We will look at these verses in this reflection.

What Love Does

What kinds of actions characterize love? The list is impressive and if we approach it with some imagination about how we feel when we act lovingly, we begin to understand what it means to be loving.

"Love is patient and kind...it rejoices at the right ...it bears all things, believes all things, hopes all things, endures all things." Now ask yourself, "When I am *patient* with someone who is really giving me a hard time, How do I do it?" You do it by making an effort to understand what is going on inside *the other* person. You do not act patiently by focusing on what is bothering you.

When you act with *kindness*, you are thinking about the suffering and needs of the other person, not your own problems.

When you *rejoice in the right*, you are happy when good things happen to others, especially to those who have been unjustly treated.

When love *bears all things* (as the English has it) it is aware that people have their own agendas in life which do not always match ours; and we let them live accordingly, even if it is somehow disconcerting to us. The Greek verb translated into the English as *bears all things* is *stego*, which means to cover something. The Greek word for roof is *stehgee;* so the action word *stego* implies roofing over, covering, protecting, defending, safeguarding, or pre-serving. Some of the Church Fathers understand the phrase *love bears all things,* to mean love covers over things; that is, love does not expose the weaknesses, failings, and sins of others. Love tries to protect others and maintain a positive attitude about others. As you see, the focus of love is on others, not ourselves.

That is also how we are to understand the phrases *"love...believes all things, hopes all things, endures all things."* These words should not be understood to mean that love is credulous, irresponsible, or passive and inactive, in some sort of general way. Those are not Christian virtues. This verse makes Christian sense when it is seen in the context of love acting in ways that focus on others, not ourselves. A paraphrase of verses six and seven written by an Orthodox theologian reads as follows:

Love is not happy when it sees people doing injustice to others, but it rejoices when it sees people being treated honestly and fairly. Love covers all the shortcomings of the neighbor, and does not parade them about. Love has good expectations in everything regarding those who are loved and believes in them and trusts them. When love sees the failings of the neighbor, it lives with the hope that the beloved person will overcome them. It readily accepts whatever is necessary to help the neighbor to overcome.

The Only Thing That Lasts

Since love acts toward other people the way God acts toward us, it is the only human thing that can last, just as God lasts for all eternity. All the important things we are, both inside and outside the Church, will end. For example, in verse eight, St. Paul noted that our prophesies (spiritual wisdom), will pass away; our teaching and our emotional religious experiences *(tongues)* will cease; even our deep and profound theological knowledge will be invalidated and come to an end.

Even now, in this life, St. Paul pointed out in verses nine through twelve, our knowledge is limited and our prophesy (spiritual instruction) is incomplete and imperfect. In this life we are like little children in all the important and significant things we do. Eventually we will give up these temporary things and grow into something more reflective of God's Kingdom.

Another image St. Paul used to make the same point is the mirror. The polished metal mirrors of antiquity never gave a clear image of the face. Like the distorted images of the bent mirrors in the amusement parks, they could never give a true representation of the person looking into them. In the last analysis, that is what all our accomplishments amount to. They are more or less distortions of the truth. Only in the end will everything be clear. In the end we will see *"face to face"* that only one thing is really permanent; only one thing makes everything else worthwhile and significant. For you see, only *"Love never ends."*

"The Greatest"

As St. Paul ends this famous chapter, he points to the three most important stars in the galaxy of God's heaven. What really counts, what really lasts, what is most significant in God's ranking of important things are these:

1. believing and trusting in Him *(faith)*

2. living with the confidence and expectation that God protects us and will fulfill all His promises about all of reality *(hope)*

3. reflecting His divine concern for each of us, in our relating to others in a way that shows concern for their welfare and their good *(love)*.

Nevertheless, St. Paul makes it clear that there is no contest over which of these three is the most excellent way: *"So faith, hope, love abide, these three; but the greatest of these is love."*

What to Aim For

Love is the most excellent way, St. Paul wrote in the last verse of chapter 12. Furthermore, he exhorts us to *"earnestly desire the higher gifts."* Important as our roles, work, and status are in the world and in the Church, the Word of God clearly teaches us that these are significant in the sight of God only when we practice them with concern for the welfare of others; not when we practice them selfishly, looking for personal gain. The Bible tells us in these two chapters in a detailed way what St. Peter tells us even more briefly: *"Finally, all of you, have unity of spirit, sympathy, love of the brethren, a tender heart and a humble mind. Do not return evil for evil or reviling for reviling; but on the contrary bless, for to this you have been called..."* (1 Pet. 3:8-9).

Even more directly and with even fewer words, the Lord Himself instructs and motivates us at the same time in regard to this greatest aspect of the Christian life: *"By this all people will know that you are my disciples, if you have love for one another"* (Jn.

13:35). Jesus' words probably inspired St. Paul to begin chapter 14 with the words, *"Make love your aim."*

The Third Gospel – Reflection 1

Apostolic Living - 1: Empowered Disciples
Matthew 10:1-8

> [1]*And he called to him his twelve disciples and gave them authority over unclean spirits, to cast them out, and to heal every disease and every infirmity.* [2]*The names of the twelve apostles are these: first, Simon, who is called Peter, and Andrew his brother; James the son of Zebedee, and John his brother;* [3]*Philip and Bartholomew; Thomas and Matthew the tax collector; James the son of Alphaeus, and Thaddaeus;* [4]*Simon the Cananaean, and Judas Iscariot, who betrayed him.*
>
> [5]*These twelve Jesus sent out, charging them, "Go nowhere among the Gentiles, and enter no town of the Samaritans,* [6]*but go rather to the lost sheep of the house of Israel.* [7]*And preach as you go, saying, 'The kingdom of heaven is at hand.'* [8]*Heal the sick, raise the dead, cleanse lepers, cast out demons. You received without paying, give without pay."*

This Gospel passage speaks of the disciples Jesus chose to be His special helpers, and to whom He eventually gave the commission to *"Go into all the world"* to preach the gospel and to establish His Church. In the verses following this passage, Jesus counsels the Twelve on how to behave toward those who welcome them and their message, and those who reject them and their message.

In these eight verses, Jesus was not speaking of the worldwide apostolic mission. Rather, He was calling His disciples to a limited, small-scale mission, like a trial run. And yet, within its limited scope, Jesus was preparing His disciples for their worldwide mission. As well, Jesus was giving us a model, for we too, in our own way, are His disciples. We will look at these eight verses in this and the following two reflections. In this reflection we will examine the first four verses to see what they have to say to us.

Jesus Empowers the Twelve

This chapter begins with the words: *"And he called to him his twelve disciples and gave them authority over unclean spirits, to cast them out and to heal every disease and every infirmity.*

What was the power Jesus gave to His disciples? Let us look at this question with some care, because it concerns us, as well. As the passage indicates, Jesus had already chosen these twelve to be his special followers. The power He gave them was similar to His own. In chapter 9 of Matthew we read *"And Jesus went about all the cities and villages, teaching in their synagogues and preaching the gospel of the kingdom, and healing every disease and every infirmity"* (v. 35). So, Jesus was preparing the Twelve to assume His work after He was gone and the Holy Spirit was to be granted to them *"in power"* to carry on the saving work of the Church.

We need to note first, that Jesus had the power because of who He was. The disciples did not and could not have this power on their own. They could not earn it. It was given to them by Christ. It was a gift.

"Unclean spirits," refer to everything that is evil and demonic. Jesus was giving the disciples the authority and power to dispel the presence and effect of evil powers, evil dispositions and, evil motiviations wherever they encountered them.

Furthermore, they were given the power to heal *"every illness and every infirmity."* The Fathers of the Church teach us that the reason for this gift of healing power was to help convince others of the truth of the message the disciples were preaching. It was the same message that Jesus preached, the good news of the Kingdom of God. One commentator, Theophylaktos, wrote, "He gives to them the power of miracles, so that they might impress those whom they would teach, thus making His audience receptive to the teaching."

Can you see that in a real sense all of us ordinary Christians are also disciples of the Lord? We are not, of course, of the same rank with the Twelve, but we are disciples, nevertheless. Through our Baptism, Chrismation, reception of the Eucharist, and membership in the Body of Christ, the Church, we too, are followers of Christ with a mission. Whatever spiritual, moral, and practical power we have against the evil in our lives is a gift from God. Whatever we accomplish is not for our own benefit, but for His glory, so that God might be worshiped, and His message proclaimed, believed, and acted upon. If we call ourselves followers of the Lord — Christians — but we display little or no power of faith, we cannot convince others of the truth of Jesus Christ.

The Disciples Named

In verses 2 through 4, Matthew wrote the names of the twelve disciples for the first time: *"Peter and Andrew, James the son of Zebedee and John, Philip and Bartholomew, Thomas and Matthew, James the son of Alphaeus and Thaddaeus, Simon the Cananaean and Judas Iscariot."*

There are some interesting characteristics to note about the apostles. First, except for the first four, we know very little about them. The apostles themselves were not nearly as important as their task. They were *apostles*, precisely because they were *sent out* (that's what the Greek means) to preach, heal, fight evil, and work for the establishment of the Kingdom. The important thing was the work they did.

Secondly, the apostles were all very different people. We often think of them as fishermen. This is true of Peter, Andrew, James, and John. However, the others did other things: Matthew was a tax collector; scholars think that Simon the Cananaean was probably originally a Zealot, a kind of political revolutionary. Each had something different to contribute.

Thirdly, these men were quite ordinary. They did not have wealth, nor were they highly-educated. They held no worldly power. They had many human weaknesses:

* Peter denied the Lord three times
* James and John egotistically sought first seats in the Kingdom and the rest were resentful of them
* Judas betrayed the Lord
* all the disciples ran away when Jesus was captured and condemned.

Yet, God forgave them and empowered them through the Holy Spirit to become the great leaders of the Church, spreading the gospel throughout the world.

Being the Lord's Disciples

Think of what God's regard for the Twelve means for us! If it is true that you and I are disciples today, even though we are mere shadows of the apostles, the same characteristics hold true for us. In the Kingdom, to be sure, the Lord knows us by name, just as He knew the Twelve by name. But they were important because of their mission and their calling.

So it is with us in the Church. We often do Church work, to be noticed, so that people will pay attention to us and give us credit. When we are motivated by selfish intentions we are missing the main point. The task is what is important. Focusing on ourselves and the credit we will get detracts from the task of advancing the work of the Church. For even the most menial and insignificant Church work we do is for the advancement of His Kingdom. That motivation should be enough for us.

The fact that all the apostles were different also points to the truth that we too are all people of different abilities and backgrounds. All of us have talents to contribute to the Kingdom. We don't have to be high and mighty, wealthy or educated, powerful and influential, or especially talented or intelligent to contribute to the work of the Kingdom. Those who have such talents should use them in God's service. All of us, however, are called to serve with whatever talents we have.

Living Apostolically

Just as Christ gave His Twelve Apostles authority to fulfill their apostolic task, in the same way, all Christians through their Baptism, Chrismation (the gift of the seal of the Holy Spirit), and participation in the Body and Blood of Christ in the Divine Liturgy are authorized to assume an apostolic mission with all the talents and abilities they have. The first step in living apostolically is to accept for yourself that you have been called as an Orthodox Christian to a life of apostolic living! The first responsibility you have when you seek to live apostolically is to recognize that your talents and abilities, whatever they are, are to be put at the service of the Kingdom of God.

Maybe it's time for each of us to make an inventory of the gifts God has given us for our own version of apostolic living!

The Third Gospel – Reflection 2

Apostolic Living 2: Apostles to Our Own
Matthew 10:1-8

¹*And he called to him his twelve disciples and gave them authority over unclean spirits, to cast them out, and to heal every disease and every infirmity.* ²*The names of the twelve apostles are these: first, Simon, who is called Peter, and Andrew his brother; James the son of Zebedee, and John his brother;* ³*Philip and Bartholomew; Thomas and Matthew the tax collector; James the son of Alphaeus, and Thaddaeus;* ⁴*Simon the Cananaean, and Judas Iscariot, who betrayed him.*

⁵*These twelve Jesus sent out, charging them, "Go nowhere among the Gentiles, and enter no town of the Samaritans,* ⁶*but go rather to the lost sheep of the house of Israel.* ⁷*And preach as you go, saying, 'The kingdom of heaven is at hand.'* ⁸*Heal the sick, raise the dead, cleanse lepers, cast out demons. You received without paying, give without pay."*

In the preceding reflection we were introduced to several facts regarding Jesus and His twelve disciples fromthe first four verses of the tenth chapter of Matthew:

* Jesus called His twelve disciples by name
* the disciples were ordinary people with all kinds of weaknesses

    * Jesus empowered the disciples by giving them authority over evil and the power to heal sickness and weaknesses.

We also saw that we too, in our own way, are disciples. God accepts us with all of our shortcomings and weaknesses, just as He did the Twelve. If we allow Him, He will empower us as well to be His disciples and His apostles to accomplish the purposes of His kingdom.

This second reflection on Matthew 10:1-8 discusses verses 5 and 6. These verses will help us to understand where it is that God calls us to work, at least at the beginning of our conscious and committed service to Him.

A Local Mission

Verses 5 and 6 are often a scandal to people. Jesus told the Twelve *"Go nowhere among the Gentiles, and enter no town of the Samaritans, but go rather to the lost sheep of the house of Israel."*

As we noted in the previous reflection, there is no reason to misunderstand these words. Later, Jesus would send His Twelve to the whole world. But here, He was sending them on a limited mission. The Greek words can be literally translated as, "Do not go upon the roads leading to pagan areas." These could easily be understood as the areas around Decapolis to the north of Galilee. Samaria was to the south of Galilee. Jesus was sending His disciples into a Jewish area, on an apostolic mission to their own people. But, it seems that their mission was even more limited than that.

On this, their first missionary journey, Jesus was sending them only to the lost sheep of the Jews in Galilee. The lost sheep in this verse are probably not the highly-educated Pharisees and Sadducees, nor the scribes and other religious leaders, but the average people who were not particularly learned in the religious law of the Jews. Therefore, in Galilee they would try out their missionary abilities among their own ordinary and common people.

The Lord's Coworkers

We must first understand that the apostles were doing Jesus Christ's work. They were following *His* work ethic. Jesus said once,

"My Father is working still, and I am working" (Jn. 5:17). Jesus made it absolutely clear to His apostles that He was doing God's work: *"So the disciples said to one another, 'Has any one brought him food?' Jesus said to them, 'My food is to do the will of him who sent me, and to accomplish his work.'"* (Jn. 4:33-35).

Jesus works. The disciples were called to work. The prophets before them worked. The implication is clear: the members of the Church of Jesus Christ are also supposed to work *"to do the will of Him who sent (us), and to accomplish His work."*

Organizational Method

If you reread the list of the apostles (Matt. 10:2-4), you will notice that the disciples are paired together in six groups. Jesus did not send them out alone, but in twos to mutually support each other and to work together. Think about that. The apostles worked together with one another. There was no private work for the Church among them. What they did, they did cooperatively with one another.

The same is true for us. The Lord's work is always fulfilled within and for the body of Christ, the Church. Do you see what that means? Working for the Church and fulfilling the tasks of the Lord require a spirit of teamwork, a sense of mutuality, and a shared vision for the overall goals and purposes of the Church.

Your Special Talents

Each of us, of course, has been given specific talents to use for the building up of the Church. Recall the parable of the talents where Jesus said, *"to one he gave five talents, to another two, to another one, to each according to his ability"* (Matt. 25:15). Each of us has gifts to place at the service of the Lord and His Church. But these personal gifts are only part of a whole picture. None of us can complete our tasks properly without reference to the other members of the Church. We need one another to do what we must do for Christ.

With this in mind, we can go back to the text and observe something very important about *our own personal* role. Jesus sent the disciples out two by two. They worked in teams. With just two in each team, there was no room for slack. Each had to pull his own weight. Thus, each partner in the two-person team had a great deal of responsibility for doing the work. This was serious work and each disciple had his hands full in order to fulfill the Master's will.

There is a famous yacht race for the America's Cup. If you've seen television accounts of the race, one of the most memorable scenes is the furious work of taking in rope and letting out sails in order to speed the ship toward the goal: winning the America's Cup. Our goal is much more important, and the need for hard and committed work for the success of the task is needed for us to fulfill our tasks for the Lord's kingdom.

In our life in the Church, we nearly always discover that there is more work to be done than there are hands to do it. If it is true that our Heavenly Father is working still and that Jesus is also working, can we do less?

Starting Close to Home With Our Own Lost Sheep

The application of these verses for you and for me and all modern-day disciples is quite clear. I'm sure you will agree that before we try to do great things for the work of the Church, we need to begin closer to home. Our own parish is the best starting place. In a spirit of love and charity, we can start with our own parish's lost sheep. No parish is without those people who have, for one reason or another, become separated from the life of the Church. We need to understand that haranguing or condemning such persons is not the right way to approach these people. The right way is the way of love.

Oftentimes, these people have been overcome by the world; its greed, its sin, its attractions. But sometimes the reason for their absence from among us is *us*. We have peculiar ways of excluding the newcomers in our parishes. Perhaps we have not given the example of Christian welcome and generosity. So, let us not be too quick to blame them for being lost sheep.

As disciples and apostles of the Lord in our home mission, we have some unique responsibilties to the lost sheep. Befriending them, speaking to them, and sharing some of our time and talents with them outside the Church hours are important ways of reaching out and showing our real interest in them. These acts of kindness as well as courteous invitations to attend Church services and various Church classes and activities with us, are far better than criticism and condemnation. Our example is most important: *what we do* is far more significant than *what we say.*

Further, we should never try to do our work for the Kingdom alone, isolated from others. The Kingdom is not a one-man or a one-woman show. Jesus sent out His disciples two-by-two. Let that be an example to us. We need to be coworkers with our priest and with one another in order to accomplish the task. It is more important that we work together in harmony than to merely complete some task. *How* we do our work for the Kingdom is even more important than *what* we do for the Kingdom.

And finally, intensity is required. God the Father works for the salvation of the world. Jesus Christ continues His saving work at the right hand of God (Eph. 1:18-23). The apostles sacrificed their lives for the sake of the Kingdom. St. Paul spoke of himself this way: *"He who plants and he who waters are equal, and each shall receive his wages according to his labor. For we are God's fellow workers . . . "* (1 Cor. 3:8-9). Elsewhere, he wrote of a number of persons who helped him in his apostolic work, describing them as *"fellow workers for the Kingdom of God"* (Col. 4:11).

So the question comes to us loud and clear. Would St. Paul refer to us as "fellow workers for the Kingdom of God"? If not, isn't it time to do something about it?

The Third Gospel – Reflection 3

Apostolic Living 3: Apostolic Work
Matthew 10:1-8

> [1]*And he called to him his twelve disciples and gave them authority over unclean spirits, to cast them out, and to heal every disease and every infirmity. *[2]*The names of the twelve apostles are these: first, Simon, who is called Peter, and Andrew his brother; James the son of Zebedee, and John his brother; *[3]*Philip and Bartholomew; Thomas and Matthew the tax collector; James the son of Alphaeus, and Thaddaeus; *[4]*Simon the Cananaean, and Judas Iscariot, who betrayed him.*
>
> [5]*These twelve Jesus sent out, charging them, "Go nowhere among the Gentiles, and enter no town of the Samaritans, *[6]*but go rather to the lost sheep of the house of Israel. *[7]*And preach as you go, saying, 'The kingdom of heaven is at hand.' *[8]*Heal the sick, raise the dead, cleanse lepers, cast out demons. You received without paying, give without pay."*

This is the last of our reflections on the first eight verses of the tenth chapter of the Gospel of Matthew. We have seen how Jesus selected His twelve disciples and assigned them to a test run missionary journey among their own people. We have also seen that He gave them the power to do the job. By drawing a modest parallel between the Twelve and us, we have come to understand our role of apostleship in our parishes, that is, the responsibility of working with one another to help bring back into active Church life those who have strayed for one reason or another. This home mission is based on love and caring, not on criticism and condemnation.

There is one final set of questions that need to be answered here. What is the message we need to bring to others? What is the apostolic work? Jesus summarized the answers to these questions in verses 7 and 8. Let's look at what He told His disciples to do.

The Meaning of the Task

"Preach as you go, saying 'The kingdom of heaven is at hand.' Heal the sick, raise the dead, cleanse lepers, cast out demons. You have received without paying, give without pay.'"

At first glance this passage seems so distant and unreal to us. I am sure that it was just as shocking and difficult for the twelve disciples to comprehend. But there is a method and a pattern to what He says. Jesus puts the priorities in order.

The Priority of the Message

The number one priority is the message. The message is about the Kingdom of God. The Kingdom of God means that we acknowledge and live in accordance with God's lordship over us in our lives. God is Lord objectively. He created the world and everything in it. Yet, He leaves us free to choose whether we will acknowledge these truths. For, you see, the Kingdom becomes real for you and me when we live our lives with full recognition in our minds, hearts, and behavior of God's will for us. Then, He is King for us. Therefore, the Kingdom must be talked about and presented to people so that they can respond. This is the first task.

Aspects of the Task

Jesus then told His disciples to *"heal the sick."* Certainly Jesus expected His twelve disciples to do healing miracles. But there is more to it than that. The Greek word for the *sick* is *astheneis*. It literally means the weak, those lacking in strength and power.

The Church has a long history of concern for the sick and their healing. From the earliest days, beginning in the New Testament, the apostles healed the sick. For example, in the New Testament book of the Acts of the Apostles there is a brief description of an apostolic healing: *"Now as Peter went here and there among them all, he came down also to the saints that lived at Lydda. There he found a man named Aeneas, who had been bedridden for eight years and was paralyzed. And Peter said to him, 'Aeneas, Jesus Christ heals you; rise and make your bed.' And immediately he rose. And all the residents of Lydda and Sharon saw him, and they turned to the Lord"* (Acts 9:32-35).

Within a few years after the apostolic period we find written prayers for the healing of the sick. People took sick people to ascetic men and women for healing. Pious physicians, like St. Panteleimon, healed the sick both with medicine and prayers, at no charge. Ill people were brought to the shrines of healing saints. Orthodox monks invented what we now call hospitals, where medicine was practiced by trained physicians who were paid by the monks to care for the poor.

Above all, the Sacrament of Holy Unction was consistently practiced through the ages. We read in the New Testament book of James the words of the institution of the healing sacrament: *"Is any among you sick? Let him call for the elders of the church, and let them pray over him, anointing him with oil in the name of the Lord; and the prayer of faith will save the sick man, and the Lord will raise him up; and if he has committed sins, he will be forgiven"* (James 5:14-15).

While using the advances of scientific medicine for ourselves and our loved ones, Christians also pray for the sick, and the restoration of health, including physical, emotional, and spiritual health.

So, healing is a practice of the Orthodox Christian faith. But healing the sick is not only giving back health to the ill, it is also making strong those who are weak. Apostolic work requires us to recognize that among us are many who feel weak and inadequate to meet the responsibilities which they must face. The apostolic task requires us to give the helping hand to those who need someone to lean on, and to give strength to those who have need of it.

"Raise the dead!" It is truly shocking that the disciples were given this task. Until then only Christ had raised anyone who was dead. But sure enough, the Bible records the raising of the dead by the apostles. The story of the raising of Tabitha (also known as Dorcas) is described in the epistle reading for the Sunday of the Paralytic:

> *Now there was at Joppa a disciple named Tabitha, which means Dorcas. She was full of good works and acts of charity. In those days she fell sick and died . . . and when (Peter) had come, they took him to the upper room. All the widows stood beside him weeping, and showing tunics and other garments which Dorcas made while she was with them. But Peter put them all outside and knelt down and prayed; then turning to the body he said, "Tabitha, rise." And she opened her eyes, and when she saw Peter she sat up. And he gave her his hand and lifted her up. Then calling the saints and widows he presented her alive. And it became known throughout all Joppa, and many believed in the Lord (Acts 9:36-43).*

It's not likely many of us could repeat a feat like that! But the dead are not only those whose bodies have died. Dead, as well, are those whose lives are spiritually and emotionally dead. We call this spiritual death. This understanding of the dead puts a new twist on what it means to raise the dead. It has practical meaning for us. Raising the dead can mean giving new hope, purpose, and spiritual vitality to the hopeless, dejected, and alienated. If we desire it, with the Lord's help, we can often give back life to those who are spiritually, morally, and emotionally dead.

"Cleanse lepers," was not only an order to the disciples to bring physical healing to these outcasts of society, but it was also a way of saying, "bring the rejected and the outsider into your membership. Include those who are otherwise excluded because of some reason which makes them unattractive to you."

Finally, as we've seen previously, *"casting out demons"* means that we are to eliminate the power and influence of evil and sin from our midst. We cast out demons by opposing the forces of darkness.

Jesus tells the Twelve not to accept payment for the work they do, other than what is necessary to maintain their life: food, clothing, and shelter. The Jewish rabbis of old would not accept payment for teaching the Law. To do so was to desecrate their calling. Clearly, Jesus was telling His disciples that the gift He was giving them was not to be used to exploit others but to help them: *"You received without paying, give without pay."* This means that the disciples should do their work motivated primarily by the desire to share the good news of the Kingdom with others and to serve them freely and openly. He does not want us to exploit each other.

Another Kind of Miracle

You can certainly see that even if you can't do miracles of the kind described in verses 7 and 8, you can reflect in your relationships with other people the miracle of changed relationships and renewed community living. As a disciple of the Lord you can strengthen the weak with whom you come into contact. You can try to inspire new life into the disheartened and spiritual purpose into the lives of the spiritually dead. You can open doors for those who are closed out of parish life (e.g., mixed marriages, the "wrong" nationality, the handicapped, those improperly excluded). You can and ought to do these things for the sake of the Kingdom, and not for any reward.

A Challenge

The first eight verses of Matthew's tenth chapter provide us with a basic lesson in apostolic living. Read the passage over and then read the balance of chapter ten in the same spirit. The apostles had their special mission. As their followers, we too share in their mission. Here we have learned to start with our own in working for God's Kingdom.

Can you make these words apply to you and your relationships with your parish? Even in some small measure? Even with just a few people? What an immense change would take place in our Orthodox parishes if we all began, even in a small way, to live in accordance to our task as disciples of the Lord!

The Fourth Epistle

Do What You Are
2 Corinthians 6:16-7:1

¹⁶What agreement has the temple of God with idols? For we are the temple of the living God; as God said, "I will live in them and move among them, and I will be their God, and they shall be my people. ¹⁷Therefore come out from them, and be separate from them, says the Lord, and touch nothing unclean; then I will welcome you, ¹⁸and I will be a father to you, and you shall be my sons and daughters, says the Lord Almighty." ¹Since we have these promises, beloved, let us cleanse ourselves from every defilement of body and spirit, and make holiness perfect in the fear of God.

What is the central message of the Bible regarding our relationship with those who are members of the Church and those who are not? The answer may be surprising to many of us...even disconcerting! There is no question that Christians are to love every person who comes across their path. But to be open to the humanity of others does not necessarily mean that our lives should be identified with every group, every mentality, every lifestyle.

St. Paul provides every Christian with guidelines for appropriate relationships with those who are not Christians, and in particular, those people whose lives embody values and practices that are not in basic harmony with God's will for human beings.

These guidelines are the subject for this reflection on 2 Corinthians 6:16-7:1.

Two Ways of Life

The setting is the early Christian Church in the city of Corinth. It appears that the Corinthian Christians were fighting among themselves. Some Corinthian Christians had forsaken their loyalty to the Church and the close bond of fellowship with the members of the body of Christ. They abandoned their relationships with fellow Christians and were associating with non-believers, with persons involved in sinful activities, and even with enemies of the Christian faith.

It is this situation that St. Paul addresses in this passage. In the verses immediately preceding, Paul calls these wayward Christians to understand the tremendous difference between the two ways of life: *"Do not be mismated with unbelievers. For what partnership have righteousness and iniquity? Or what fellowship has light with darkness? What accord has Christ with Belial? Or what has a believer in common with an unbeliever?"*

On the one hand are righteousness, light, Christ, and the believer. On the other are iniquity (sin), darkness, Belial (the devil), and unbelievers. St. Paul is clearly asking his Corinthian readers to understand that there is something fundamentally different about a Christian that creates a line of separation between the kind of life he or she lives and the kind of life the unbeliever lives. In this passage St. Paul is not writing about casual or ordinary behavior. In fact, St. Paul himself dealt with all kinds of people as a tentmaker and he appealed to Roman authorities. Furthermore, he instructed the Christians of Rome, *"If possible, so far as it depends upon you, live peaceably with all"* (Rom. 12:18).

In this passage St. Paul was referring to behavior that is contrary to Christian teaching, and would compromise the Christian's identity as one who had *"put on Christ"* (Rom. 13:14, Gal. 3:27) and who had *"put on the new man"* (Eph. 4:24, Col. 3:10). According to St. Paul, associating with people who were immoral and did unethical things was clearly wrong for the Christian, as was associating with pagan religious practices that would compromise one's standing as a Christian.

St. Paul is consciousness raising here. His message to you and me is that we need to always be aware of who we are: members of God's household, baptized so that the old man has died, and the new man resurrected in us is part of God's own people, His Church.

You Are the Temple of God

In this passage St. Paul seems to have in mind Christians who were somehow involving themselves in practices associated with pagan worship. Our passage begins with these words: "What agreement has the temple of God with idols? For we are the temple of the living God."

Pagan temples had restaurants connected to them. These eating places served the meats that had been offered to the pagan gods on the altars of the pagan temple. Pagans would invite people to these temple restaurants, just as easily as you might invite a friend to have lunch with you at a nice restaurant today. "I invite you to dine with me at the table of our Lord Serapis," might be the form of an invitation. St. Paul's response is that the acceptance of such an invitation might compromise one's identity as a Christian.

Elsewhere, in the eighth chapter of 1 Corinthians, St. Paul argued that Christians should not eat in such places because they might scandalize other Christians. Here, he seems to be saying that it is inappropriate to do this or anything else that would compromise one's own Christian identity.

For Christians today, the translation is easy. The moral equivalents of the pagan temples are all around us. What business do Christians have patronizing movie theatres that show pornographic films? What agreement is there between those who have received the Spirit of God and the taking of illicit narcotics and drugs? How can we maintain our identity as Christians and go to plays that blaspheme God? Unfortunately, the examples in our modern secular culture are legion. St. Paul is teaching us here that our behavior has to be in harmony with our identity as Christians.

Separate Yourself!

St. Paul used the image of Christians as temples of God in his first letter to the Corinthians when he wrote the powerful statement: *"Do you not know that you are God's temple and that God's Spirit dwells in you? If anyone destroys* (Greek, *phtheirei*, which translated means corrupts) *God's temple, God will destroy him. For God's temple is holy, and that temple you are"* (1 Cor. 3:16-17). St. Paul may have been thinking of the Old Testament King Manasseh who defiled the temple of Jerusalem by bringing an idol into it (2 Kings 21:1-9; Septuagint 4 Kingdoms 21:1-9) when he phrased this teaching in this way.

Here, however, St. Paul develops this idea of the Christian as a temple of God in a positive way. Apparently from memory, St. Paul recollects an entire collection of Old Testament sayings which he compiles into a series of observations about Christians being the temple of God, and what that means. It seems that he is referring to the basic ideas in passages such as Leviticus 26:11,12; Isaiah 52:11; Ezekiel 20:34; 37:27, and 2 Samuel 7:14.

Verses 16b, 17 and 18 give us the implications of the truth that Christians are *"the temple of the living God."* These implications are:

* We are *"God's people"* and God *"lives in (us)"* and *"moves among (us).""*
* There is a separation from Christians and those who live in ways that are in direct contradiction to the goodness and purity of God. We are to *"touch nothing unclean."*
* If we act correctly, we will strengthen the bond between ourselves and God. In that case, God says "I will welcome you, and I will be a father to you, and you shall be my sons and daughters."

Make Holiness Perfect

Another word for this separation from sinful and evil behavior, circumstances, environment, and company is holiness. The conclusion, then, calls us to repentance for our failures in this matter in the past: *"let us cleanse ourselves from every defilement of body and spirit."* No matter what we have done in the past, if we are willing to correct the situation, to start anew, and to struggle to separate ourselves from evil and sin, God is ready to receive our repentance and to reestablish us as full members of His household.

This message is not for some supposedly perfect and sinless Christians, but for each and every one of us. Repentance is the way we get back on track, and it is available to each of us on a daily basis *("forgive us our trespasses...")*, and, when we are dealing with something more serious, through the Sacrament of Holy Confession.

Finally, our goal and our task is summarized in St. Paul's words *"make holiness perfect in the fear of God." The Greek is epitelountes aghiosyne*, which literally means, accomplishing and fulfilling holiness.

Do What You Are!

Do you see what St. Paul is saying? "You are a child of God who has been redeemed by Christ so that you are now a member of the Lord's Kingdom and are no longer under the dominion of sin and evil. You are the temple of the living God." As a result, he is saying to you, "Act like it." Manifest the fact that you are God's temple. Fulfill the reality that you belong to God in the way you live your life. This passage of the Bible says to you: "Don't associate with things and events and people that are opposed to what you are. Rather, *do* what you *are!"*

The Fourth Gospel Reflection 1

Never Without Help
Matthew 8:14-17

> ¹⁴*And when Jesus entered Peter's house, he saw his mother-in-law lying sick with a fever;* ¹⁵*he touched her hand, and the fever left her, and she rose and served him.* ¹⁶*That evening they brought to him many who were possessed with demons; and he cast out the spirits with a word, and healed all who were sick.* ¹⁸*This was to fulfil what was spoken by the prophet Isaiah, "He took our infirmities and bore our diseases."*

Rare is the person who has never felt abandoned by his or her family and friends, who has never experienced weakness and failure, who has never borne loss, disillusionment, or betrayal, or suffered physical or emotional hurt. Such a person, I'm sure you'll agree, is rare indeed. Frankly, I don't believe I have ever met such a person!

Everyone I have met in my years in the priesthood has experienced, in one way or another, all of those struggles and more. What is more terrible than the struggles themselves, is having to face them alone. Fortunately, the Christian does not have to face these difficulties alone. The Christian, like everyone else, will have to face difficulties in life, but never alone, never without help. Why? Because the Christian has Christ. A story of healing from the Gospel of Matthew helps us to understand this tremendous supportive truth.

A Busy Day For Jesus

The way Matthew tells it, a long and busy day was nearing its end when the events described in Matthew 8:14-17 took place. In the morning, Jesus had given His famous Sermon on the Mount. Afterwards, crowds of people followed him. In one of the crowds there was a leper who came and asked Jesus to heal him of his illness. Jesus did. Then, as Jesus was returning to Capernaum, where He was staying at Peter's house, the virtuous and humble Centurian, an officer of the Roman army, approached Jesus and asked him to heal his paralyzed servant. Jesus did with just a word.

Finally, the Lord and His disciples arrived at Peter's house. Perhaps it would now be possible to get some rest! But no, it was not to be. Jesus would have to deal with another illness. Matthew describes the situation: *"And when Jesus entered Peter's house, he saw his mother-in-law lying sick with a fever; he touched her hand and the fever left her, and she rose and served him."*

Commentators think it was likely that Peter's mother-in-law had malaria, a common illness in the area of Capernaum and Tiberias in those days. Even when a person was fortunate enough to get over the illness, a long period of recuperation followed. Strength was regained slowly. From Matthew's account of this healing we can't tell if Peter's mother-in-law asked for healing or not. However, from the accounts of the same miracle in Mark and Luke (Mark 1:29-31; Luke 4:38-39), it is obvious that the other disciples, probably not Peter himself, told Jesus about her illness and asked Jesus to heal her. Luke says *"they besought him for her"* (Luke 4:38).

Whatever the case, the remarkable thing to note is Jesus' immediate willingness to help. *"He touched her hand,"* and she was miraculously cured. Not only did her high fever leave her immediately, but she suffered none of the debilitating weaknesses that follow an illness like malaria.

Christ Is There To Help

Peter's mother-in-law was suffering and she needed help. Whether she asked for it herself or whether it was the result of the entreaties of the other disciples, Jesus was there to help. Tired and exhausted as He was, as a human being, from the many burdens of the day's activities, there was no hesitation on His part to help. In our pain, our suffering, our discomfort, our hurt, Christ is always there, ready to help. Do you see what that means? *We are never alone!*

All Kinds and Everyone

But the day was not over. For you see, it seems as though these miracles were taking place on the Sabbath! According to the Mosaic law, as interpreted by the rabbis, all that had been done this day was against the religious law! Many of the observant Jews who wanted Jesus' help had not approached him during the day for this reason. They waited until evening. When they saw the first two stars in the early evening sky, the Sabbath was officially over. Now they could approach the Lord!

So, *"that evening they brought to him many who were possessed with demons; and he cast out the spirits with a word and healed all who were sick."* Peter's mother-in-law had a physical illness. Here we see what is commonly called in our day emotional or mental illness. Both physical illness and emotional disorder are brought before Jesus on this day for healing.

It was night when people usually rested, even the Lord. But here He was, curing and helping people in need. They crowded around him. The friends and relatives of the sick called out, implored, pushed, and shoved to come close to the Great Physician. And, *"He healed all who were sick!"*

It Was His Mission

Matthew now reveals to us why he tells these stories of Jesus' readiness to comfort and heal all manner of people. On this day, Jesus exercised spiritual healing through His teaching in the Sermon on the Mount. He then healed the outcast leper, the servant of a powerful and feared military authority, a relative of one of His disciples, and crowds of ordinary people. No class of people remains excluded from His healing care! Quoting the Hebrew version of Is. 53:4, Matthew shows that Jesus did all these things because He fulfills one of the roles of the Messiah as the prophesies tell: *"This was to fulfill what was spoken by the prophet Isaiah, 'He took our infirmities and bore our diseases.'"*

Think about that. One of the reasons Christ came into the world was to take up our weaknesses and to bear our illnesses! It was part of His mission to help us, to support us, to remove from us the bitterness and the hurt each of us experiences. Now we understand why on that day long, long ago in Capernaum, Jesus never stopped helping people. You see, it was then, and still is, an important part of His mission.

Lessons For Us

We learn some important lessons from these verses. First, we are *never alone* in our pain and suffering. Do you remember what we hear at Christmastime? One of the names given to Jesus Christ was *"Emmanuel."* This is what the Gospel of Matthew says about that name: *"Behold the virgin will conceive and bear a Son, and his name will be called Emmanuel, which means, God with us"* (Matt. 1:23).

For believers in Jesus Christ, the greatest comfort we can have in times of trouble, pain, sorrow, and trial is the remembrance that God is always with us. Just as the air surrounds us, He is beside us always. Invisible, but present. Life giving, but not intruding. It is up to us to draw the air into our lungs. In a similar way, it is up to us to bring ourselves consciously into His presence.

Secondly, we must *call upon Him* for help, no matter how unworthy we might feel. Christ has given us a tremendous promise, if we will turn our attention to Him. Listen to these words: *"And I tell you, ask, and it will be given you; seek, and you will find; knock, and it will be opened to you. For every one who asks receives, and he who seeks finds, and to him who knocks it will be opened"* (Lk. 11:9-10).

Isn't that remarkable? The Lord of the universe is ready to listen to us any time of the day or night, in our joy and in our sorrow, in our pain and in our suffering. In the Orthodox way of living, we have been taught the Jesus Prayer, that is, to *"pray without ceasing,"* or as another translation puts it, to *"pray con-*

stantly," (1 Thess. 5:17) invoking the name of Jesus Christ. Prayer is a key to opening ourselves to the living, healing, comforting presence of the Lord.

Thirdly, there is a secret truth here. Even in our suffering we need to remember others. We need to *keep our eye out for others* who need His help. The Christian learns to find strength in his or her own suffering by praying for others. Don't wait for everything to be fine with you before you pray for others in their need. The secret is: when we are lovingly concerned about others we draw pain away from ourselves!

Next, God heals and comforts us to *be of service to others.* In the fourth century, St. Gregory the Theologian, a great father of the Church, wrote about his friend St. Basil. This other great father of the Church had established a complex of philanthropic institutions in the city of Caesaria of the province of Cappadocia, where he was bishop. St. Gregory wrote, "It was (Basil), above all, who urged us not to despise our fellows or to dishonor Christ, the one Head of all of us, by our inhumanity to them, but in the misfortunes of others to consult well our own interests, and to lend to God the mercy of which we stand in need ourselves." By seeing the misfortunes of others and seeking to help others, we are comforted ourselves.

Lastly, *never forget* that *"He took our infirmities and bore our diseases"* (Matt. 8:17). Thank God for that!

The Christian is *never* without help! Ask in the right way, and it shall be given to you!

The Fourth Gospel – Reflection 2

What It Takes To Be A Follower of Christ
Matthew 8:18-22

> ^{18}*Now when Jesus saw great crowds around him, he gave orders to go over to the other side.* ^{19}*And a scribe came up and said to him, "Teacher, I will follow you wherever you go."* ^{20}*And Jesus said to him, "Foxes have holes, and birds of the air have nests; but the Son of man has nowhere to lay his head."* ^{21}*Another of the disciples said to him, "Lord, let me first go and bury my father."* ^{22}*But Jesus said to him, "Follow me, and leave the dead to bury their own dead."*

By name, Christians are identified as followers of Christ. The Bible tells us that the disciples of Christ were given the name of Christians in Antioch (Acts 11:26). Jesus frequently spoke about what it meant to follow Him. It would take many volumes to explore all the references to discipleship in the New Testament.

In the passage we are going to look at in this and the next reflection, Jesus confronts two would-be disciples. How he deals with them teaches us a great deal about what it takes to be a follower of Christ. We will discover that discipleship is both costly and demanding.

The Lord Who Commands

"Now when Jesus saw great crowds around him, he gave orders to go over to the other side" (Matt. 8:18).

Jesus gave orders. He spoke and the sick were healed. He ordered and nature obeyed. He commanded and His disciples followed. But in this passage, before Jesus entered the boat with His disciples to cross the Sea of Galilee, two of Jesus' possible followers approached Him and tested Jesus about what it would mean to follow Him.

The candidates were totally different from each other and they both, it seems, failed to make the grade. In a few verses we meet the first of them, a scribe who claimed to want to be a follower of the Lord. Let us look at Jesus' encounter with him to learn something about what it means to be a follower of Christ.

On The Lord's Terms Only

"And a scribe came up and said to him, 'Teacher, I will follow you wherever you go.' And Jesus said to him, 'Foxes have holes and birds of the air have nests; but the Son of man has nowhere to lay his head'" (Matt. 8:19-20).

The scribes were among the most learned persons in Jewish society at the time. They (the Greek word for scribe is *grammateus,* which literally means he who writes) were scholars of the Hebrew Scriptures, the Torah. They were well-educated teachers who held great prestige and respect among the people, and could be compared to ordained theologians of today.

Jesus, of course, was not counted as being among them. They thought Jesus was unlearned in the Law. Most of the scribes criticized Jesus and condemned His teaching (Matt. 9:3; 15:2; 21:15).

But here was one who claimed to believe in Christ and said that he wanted to follow Him. St. John Chrysostom points out that Jesus didn't look only to the words the man said, but also understood his inner disposition, his intentions. This offer of the scribe is like a man with a Ph.D. offering to become the follower of a storefront preacher. Can you imagine what the scholar's attitude would be?

The Inner Disposition

Hidden in his words were condescension and pride. "Do you see how great his arrogance is?" asks Chrysostom, "He comes near, not deigning to be numbered with the multitude, thereby indicating that he is above the common sort." His motives did not appear on the surface. But with his high scholarly standing, Jesus suspects the scribe wants to be a disciple, but only on *his* terms. The scholar needs his books, library, desk, study, scholarly resources, quiet, and leisure. The scribe wants to follow, but only in a way that suits him. That is simply not what it means to be a disciple.

So, Jesus puts him to the test. Is the desire to be a disciple complete? Is it sincere? "Sure," Jesus says in effect, "you can become my disciple, but you will not be able to do it on your terms. You will not be able to continue being an authority, a teacher of the people, and a scholar. You will not be able to stay put in your comfortable study, making authoritative statements about the Law. For if you are going to follow Me you must abandon your style of life and assume mine."

"Foxes have their holes, and birds of the air have nests; but the Son of man has nowhere to lay his head." The following can be said about a true follower of Jesus: "Who you are, where you are, what you do, no longer defines you. Your discipleship to Me must become the most important thing about your life." This is what Jesus was saying to this proud man.

Like the rich young ruler who turned away from Jesus when wealth stood in the way of discipleship (Matt. 22:26; Lk. 20:25), the scribe failed to rise to the occasion: Chrysostom sadly noted that "he did not say, 'I am ready to follow You.'" His pride of position and intellectual arrogance kept him out of the number of the disciples. He wanted discipleship on his own terms, and the lesson we learn is that there is no such thing.

His Terms; Not Yours

To be a Christian is to be a follower of Christ. To be a follower of Christ means many things. If we are Christians in heart, mind, and spirit, and not in name only, these lines of

Scripture challenge us. To follow Christ on His terms, not our own, means that we are ready to see His will in the circumstances surrounding us.

In St. Paul's letter to the Philippians the relationship between those who would follow Jesus Christ as Lord is made abundantly clear:

> *God has highly exalted him and bestowed on him the name which is above every name, that at the name of Jesus every knee should bow, in heaven and on earth and under the earth, and every tongue confess that Jesus Christ is Lord, to the glory of God the Father (Phil. 2:9-11).*

In today's terms, we would say that Jesus is our "boss." Because He is our boss, you and I need to be attentive to His expectations of us. We do what He tells us to do because we are in His service and employ.

We Christians need to acknowledge that Christ is our Lord. Do you see what that means? We Christians are followers of Christ only insofar as we think, talk, and act in ways that reveal full loyalty, devotion, commitment, and obedience to Christ. Otherwise, our Christian identity is weak and unfulfilled.

Where Do You Stand?

You may remember that in the Divine Liturgy and in many of the other worship services of the Orthodox Church, a particular liturgical expression is repeated numerous times: "Let us commit ourselves and one another and our whole life to Christ our God." I once reminded a parishioner who had been influenced by a Protestant evangelist, of this expression, when he asked, "Why doesn't the Orthodox Church have altar calls"? The so-called altar call is based on a theology of salvation that is foreign to the Orthodox Church, but the call to commit ourselves to Christ is not. During the Divine Liturgy this invitation is extended about eight times. But the difficulty of translation obscures something dramatic about the way the invitation is extended.

The Greek word translated as *commit* or even less intensely, to *commend* ourselves to Christ, is much more powerful than the attitude or actions conveyed by the English. The Greek word is *parathometha* and it comes from the root verb *paratithimi.* This word consists of two simpler words, *tithimi,* which means to "place oneself" or to "position oneself," and *para,* which means next to or alongside someone or something.

So a literal translation would be something like this: "let us stand beside Christ," "let us be on Christ's side," or "let us stand up next to Christ." In military terms, you could understand the literal translation to mean becoming a soldier in Christ's spiritual army.

You get the picture. This much-repeated invitation requires us to make a conscious choice about whose side we are on in the struggle between evil and good, the demonic and the divine, the devil and God. We are repeatedly called upon, not only in the Divine Liturgy, but practically from minute to minute, to choose between what some of the earliest Christian writers called "the way of death or the way of Life." When we stand on Christ's side we declare to ourselves and to everyone who will see that we are Christ's, members of His body, His Church.

So there it is! Where do you stand? You are repeatedly called to stand beside Christ in one situation and circumstance after the other. How do you respond? What choice do you make? The Divine Liturgy extends the invitation "Let us take our place next to Christ our God, on His side, as His committed followers . . . ." So a Christian, in heart, mind, and spirit, and not in name only, doesn't serve the Lord on his or her conditions, but on the Lord's conditions.

This service to Christ on His terms and conditions is the first of two true marks of discipleship which are highlighted in Matt. 8:18-22. In our next reflection we will look at the other.

The Fourth Gospel – Reflection 3

The "Why" of Following Christ
Matthew 8:18-23

> [18]*Now when Jesus saw great crowds around him, he gave orders to go over to the other side.* [19]*And a scribe came up and said to him, "Teacher, I will follow you wherever you go." * [20]*And Jesus said to him, "Foxes have holes, and birds of the air have nests; but the Son of man has nowhere to lay his head." * [21]*Another of the disciples said to him, "Lord, let me first go and bury my father." * [22]*But Jesus said to him, "Follow me, and leave the dead to bury their own dead."*
>
> [23]*And when he got into the boat, his disciples followed him.*

Being a follower of Jesus, a Christian, is a total experience. It requires full devotion, loyalty, and commitment. In the previous reflection, we looked at these words from the eighth chapter of Matthew:

"And a scribe came up and said to him, 'Teacher, I will follow you wherever you go.' And Jesus said to him, 'Foxes have holes and birds of the air have nests; but the Son of man has nowhere to lay his head'" (Matt. 8:19-20).

We saw in the preceding reflection the scribe's error: he wanted to be a follower of Jesus on his own terms. The scholar's requirement that he be settled, with his books in his study, was not compatible with the travelling ministry of the Lord. We came to understand that if we are to be genuine disciples of the Lord, we must follow Him wherever *He* wants us to serve. There is another important truth affirmed for us in this passage. This truth is the reason why it is right and proper for us to be the Lord's disciples in the first place.

"The Son of Man"

In this passage Jesus called Himself *"the Son of Man."* There are several levels of meaning to this phrase that would have been meaningful to the scribe. On the first level, Jesus identified Himself with all human beings. He is a *"son of Mary"* (Mk. 6:3), born like all other human beings, sharing in the human condition. But here, as in all other places where Christ used this phrase about Himself, He always used the word *the.* He is not only *a* human being . . . Jesus is *the* human being.

In other words, Jesus is the new Adam, who is the redeemer and savior of the world! The name *Adam* in Hebrew literally means *human being.* So now you can understand what St. Paul meant when he wrote in his first letter to the Corinthians: *". . .as by a man came death (the first Adam), by a man (Jesus Christ) has come the resurrection of the dead"* And, *"the first man Adam became a living being; the last Adam became a life-giving spirit"* (15:22,45).

The prophet Daniel spoke of the *Son of Man* as well. Here is what he said:

> *I saw in the night visions, and behold,*
> *with the clouds of heaven*
> *there came one like a son of man*
> *and he came to the Ancient of Days*
> *and was presented before him.*
>
> *And to him was given dominion and*
> *glory and Kingdom,*
> *that all peoples, nations, and languages*
> *should serve him;*

> *His dominion is an everlasting dominion,*
> *which shall not pass away,*
> *and his kingdom*
> *one that shall not be destroyed. (Dan. 7:13-14)*

Jesus Christ, the Son of Man, is also the Son of God! To Him, the *Ancient of Days*, that is, the first person of the Holy Trinity, the Father, has given the Son, Jesus Christ, eternal dominion over the creation, manifesting the divine in the created. This manifestation of the divine in the created is a definition of the Kingdom of God. The Kingdom of God is fulfilled when *"all peoples, nations, and languages should serve him."* But unlike the kingdoms of this world, it is not imposed by force, but awaits our voluntary commitment. We are, as Orthodox worship declares, called to freely, voluntarily, and personally "commit ourselves and one another and our whole life to Christ our God."

The First Christian Creed

The phrase *"Jesus Christ is Lord,"* or *"Jesus is Lord,"* appears in three places in the New Testament. Scholars believe that the appearance of this phrase is more than chance. Christians first summarized their faith with this phrase, it was the first Christian Creed! St. Paul pointed to the need for believers to *"confess with your lips that Jesus is Lord"* (Rom. 10:9).

To confess that *Jesus Christ is Lord* is the spiritual equivalent of drawing a line in the sand. It says that the whole Church, and you with it, acknowledge Jesus Christ as the most important reality in life. It is a life-defining statement. When we recognize Jesus Christ as Lord, everything He stands for, the world-view with God at the top, and the values leading to God-likeness, become the standard for us. It means that communion with God the Father through Jesus Christ in the Holy Spirit is the essence of life. It means that we live our lives, make our decisions, orient ourselves to the events of the day, and guide our decisions by acknowledging that *Jesus Christ is Lord.*

We are taught by the Word of God that saying those words sincerely and with faithful commitment is a sign that we are already standing on Christ's side *(parathometha)*, because no one can make that statement of faithful commitment without already being inspired by the Holy Spirit. It is a question of your fundamental orientation in life. You are either on Christ's side, or on the devil's side. This is how St. Paul put it: *"Therefore I want you to understand that no one speaking by the Spirit of God ever says 'Jesus be cursed!' and no one can say 'Jesus is Lord' except by the Holy Spirit"* (1 Cor. 12:3).

We recognize Jesus Christ as Lord (King, Ruler, Chief, Commander, Head, Boss, Leader, Master) of our lives, because according to the Christian faith, He *is* Lord in reality! The Bible expresses this truth in a powerful way:

> *Therefore God has highly exalted*
> *him and bestowed on him the name which*
> *is above every name,*
> *that at the name of Jesus every*
> *knee should bow, in heaven and on earth*
> *and under the earth, and every tongue confess that*
> *Jesus Christ is Lord, to the glory of God*
> *the Father (Phil. 2:9-11).*

Why should we follow Jesus? Why should He be our Lord? Why should Christians who believe in Jesus Christ as Savior obey His commandments, call Him Lord, and serve Him with their total being? You are entitled to ask those questions. Here is the answer. Because it is the most fitting and appropriate thing for human beings to do. "To him was given dominion and glory and Kingdom, that all peoples, nations and languages should serve him." Not on our terms, but on His, not just *when WE want to serve,* but *when HE wants us to serve!*

When He Wants; Not When We Want

"Another of the disciples said to him, 'Lord, let me first go and bury my father.' But Jesus said to him, 'Follow me, and leave the dead to bury their own dead'" (Matt. 8:21-22).

This phrase seems to be harsh when we first read it. It is hard for us to imagine that Jesus would refuse a man the duty of burying his dead father. We think that only when we don't understand this Middle Eastern way of speaking.

Some time ago, a Christian missionary became friendly with a wealthy young Turkish man. He encouraged him to further his education, to travel, and to broaden his understanding of the world. The Turk, however, refused. In justification, he said "I must first of all bury my father." When the missionary started to offer condolences, the young man explained that his father had not died. Rather, he couldn't pursue his education until he had fulfilled all of his duties to his parents and relatives. "I certainly want to be educated through this travel which you suggest," he said, "but it will have to wait."

When the man told Jesus, *"Let me first go and bury my father,"* he was procrastinating. He felt the call, but he didn't want to follow when Christ was calling. He wanted to do it at his own convenience, when he was ready. Jesus' apparently harsh words about the "dead burying their own dead," had nothing to do with funerals!

Rather, Jesus was saying that obedience to His call can't be postponed. When our hearts are touched by the call to follow Him and do His will, and we don't say "yes," we may well have lost for good the opportunity to serve Him. The young Turk never did complete his education. Many who have felt the call to the priesthood and postponed it, have found themselves regretting their hesitancy years later. The occasion for an act of kindness or philanthropy, if postponed, is often lost forever. The word of the Lord ignored today may never have an opportunity for fulfillment again.

Discipleship is not on our time, it is on the Lord's time. He provides the occasions; He opens the door for service; He presents before us the opportunity to serve. Following the Lord means seizing the moment. It means not giving excuses, not postponing, not procrastinating. It means saying "Yes!" to the Lord's prompting to serve Him. Now! Right where we are! In the particular circumstances He has called us!

When, Where, How He Wants

To be a Christian is to be a follower of Christ. If we are Christians in heart, mind, and spirit, and not in name only, these words of Jesus challenge us. You follow Christ because He is Lord in the full meaning of that word. That means you need to follow Him and be ready to see His will in whatever circumstances surround you. This choice to follow Him is not imposed upon you. It is a choice you must make. That is why He said, *"Whosoever would come after me, let him take up his cross and follow me"* (Matt. 16:24).

A Christian in heart, mind, and spirit, and not in name only, doesn't serve the Lord on his or her conditions, but on the Lord's conditions.

A Christian in heart, mind, and spirit, and not in name only, doesn't serve the Lord only where he or she wants, but wherever the Lord requires.

A Christian in heart, mind, and spirit, and not in name only, doesn't serve the Lord just when it's convenient to him or her, but when the Lord requires. These are marks of true discipleship, to serve when, where, and how the Lord wills.

The Essential Step

Few of us measure up to these standards, but we should continue to strive to reach that level of commitment. Our Lord knows how difficult it is for us. In His human nature He shared in our human passions and condition. That makes His Lordship even more remarkable. He knows our weaknesses because He suffered them, yet He remains Lord of the universe! It is easier for us to struggle to grow toward Godlikeness when we remember that the Lord of the universe shared in the struggles of our human condition.

So it is that in the New Testament book of Hebrews we read: *"Therefore he (Jesus) had to be made like his brethren (us) in every respect, so that he might become a merciful and faithful high priest in the service of God, to make expiation for the sins of the people. For because he himself has suffered and been tempted, he is able to help those who are tempted"* (Heb. 2:17-18).

The essential step is to acknowledge Jesus Christ as Lord of *your* life. The rest follows.

St. Athanasius, in one of his writings against the Arians, summarizes what these last two reflections have sought to express:

> *The one to whom the passions are ascribed, in particular the condemnation, scourging, thirst, crucifixion and death, together with the other weaknesses of the body, is the same as he to whom the triumph and the grace belong. It is thus consistent and appropriate to ascribe these passions to the Lord and not to someone else. For then the grace also will come from him, and our worship will not be directed to anyone else. We shall be truly religious, since the one whom we invoke is no creature, no ordinary man, but the true and natural Son of God, who also became man and yet is no less Lord and God and Saviour.*

The passage ends with the words "his disciples followed him." That's the way it is!

The Fifth Epistle

Afflictions
2 Corinthians 1:8-11

⁸For we do not want you to be ignorant, brethren, of the affliction we experienced in Asia; for we were so utterly, unbearably crushed that we despaired of life itself. ⁹Why, we felt that we had received the sentence of death; but that was to make us rely not on ourselves but on God who raises the dead; ¹⁰he delivered us from so deadly a peril, and he will deliver us; on him we have set our hope that he will deliver us again. ¹¹You also must help us by prayer, so that many will give thanks on our behalf for the blessing granted us in answer to many prayers.

My dictionary defines the word *affliction* as:

1. State of being afflicted. **2.** the cause of continued pain of body, or mind, as illness, losses, etc.; also a grievous distress. — Syn. Trial, tribulation, visitation, cross.

You don't need to have all the details when you hear that someone has suffered some affliction, to know that it wasn't pleasant, or easy, or comfortable. In this short passage from his second letter to the Christians of Corinth, St. Paul wrote about a serious affliction he suffered. He reflects on the affliction and he lets us know how he was helped to overcome it. These verses provide us with some powerful inspiration for meeting, understanding, and addressing the afflictions that come into our lives.

"Utterly, Unbearably Crushed"

"We do not want you to be ignorant, brethren, of the affliction we experienced in Asia; for we were so utterly, unbearably crushed that we despaired of life itself."

St. Paul commonly shared his personal experiences with the brethren (1 Cor. 10:1; 12:1; Rom. 1:13; 11:25). *"We do not want you ignorant, brethren..."* He didn't keep these events to himself. You see, he wanted his beloved Corinthian Christians to know what happened to him. Sharing spiritual struggles and insights is an apostolic example for us.

Tell your spouse, family members, and friends about your spiritual concerns, struggles, defeats, and victories. But most important of all, have the confidence to share these things with your spiritual father. In the one case, you help impress others with the importance of the spiritual life. In the other, your priest can support and guide you. In any case, you ought not try to face trials and tribulations in life alone.

Thlipsis is the Greek word St. Paul used which is translated as *affliction*. The NIV translates *thlipsis* as *hardships*. Its primary meaning, however, is to be squeezed down, to be under pressure. Something happened to St. Paul which was so serious and so painful that he felt it was like a huge rock or boulder on him. He felt that he was utterly, unbearably crushed.

It seems that he asked himself if he would ever get out from under, whether he would ever escape from the situation, whether he would survive it. The response was devastating. *"We despaired of life itself."* When he looked to his own abilities to overcome, there was no hope. Here we see a saint of God who is pushed to the extreme. Since the particular situation that brought Paul and his companions to despair is not mentioned, we must assume that it was recently experienced and was known to the Corinthian congregation. Here, Paul told them how serious it was.

How often you and I have felt this kind of weight in our lives! When defeat of our hopes and dreams seems ready to overtake us, we know well that sense of being weighed down. We know the heavy weight of *thlipsis.* How easy it is to fall into despair! But St. Paul wants to show us how to overcome despair.

Who Lifts the Weight?

"Why, we felt that we had received the sentence of death." Once the death sentence is pronounced, the criminal can do nothing more for himself. He is at the mercy of others. St. Paul knew that alone, he could do nothing to free himself from this terrible affliction. Someone else had to give him the reprieve. And that someone else is God! Paul was pushed to turn to the Lord to find release from his suffering. *"...but that was to make us rely not on ourselves, but on God who raises the dead."* Don't you see? God has the power precisely because He is the victor over death, sin, and every evil!

The message of this passage is a call to believe in God who can overcome our every affliction. To believe this in your heart is the first step in overcoming the crushing burdens of life. Believe it! God can lift the weight!

God is Always Our Support

"He delivered us from so deadly a peril, and he will deliver us; on him we have set our hope that he will deliver us again."

As St. Paul faced these afflictions of life with the help of God, he was taught to put his trust in the Lord. His past experiences gave him confidence about facing the future. How deliberate and firm he sounds! *"We have set our hope that he (God) will deliver us again."* In the eighth chapter of his letter to the Romans, St. Paul stated this conviction with real power:

"We know that in everything God works for good with those who love him."

"If God is for us, who is against us?"

"Who shall separate us from the love of Christ? Shall tribulation, or distress, or persecution, or famine, or nakedness or peril, or sword?...No, in all

these things we are more than conquerors through him who loved us."

We should repeat these three verses of hope and strength when we, like St. Paul, experience crushing afflictions in our lives. In God, no matter what comes to us, we have the strength of hope. These are words of strength and power for the Christian believer. They can help you in times of affliction. Copy them down. Carry them with you. Repeat them whenever you feel the weight of affliction in your life.

God gives us another source of help, too. Let us see what St. Paul now adds.

Strength From Each Other

What will provoke this help from God? Yes, Paul prayed to God for himself. But he knew that the prayers of his beloved Corinthian Christians were also necessary. *"You must help us by prayer"*, he told them. At the beginning of this reflection we noted how St. Paul shared the experiences of his suffering with his fellow Christians. Here, he tells them that because they now know of his afflictions, they are obligated, as fellow Christians, to pray for him in his need.

How often, when we hear of the afflictions of some neighbor or family member or fellow parishioner, we feel helpless. We say "I wish I could do something!" We are instructed here that we can *always* do something: we can pray. And when God answers (no matter how He answers), our prayers give us the opportunity to join in thanksgiving to Him. We must pray for those in affliction, as St. Paul concludes *"so that many will give thanks on our behalf for the blessing granted us in answer to many prayers."*

There it is. Afflictions will certainly come to us. But we are never alone, never helpless. We have God, and we have each other.

The Fifth Gospel

Ready for the Coming of the Lord?
Matthew 25:1-13

¹Then the kingdom of heaven shall be compared to ten maidens who took their lamps and went to meet the bridegroom. ²Five of them were foolish, and five were wise. ³For when the foolish took their lamps, they took no oil with them; ⁴but the wise took flasks of oil with their lamps. ⁵As the bridegroom was delayed, they all slumbered and slept. ⁶But at midnight there was a cry, "Behold, the bridegroom! Come out to meet him." ⁷Then all those maidens rose and trimmed their lamps. ⁸And the foolish said to the wise, "Give us some of your oil, for our lamps are going out." ⁹But the wise replied, Perhaps there will not be enough for us and for you; go rather to the dealers and buy for yourselves." ¹⁰And while they went to buy, the bridegroom came, and those who were ready went in with him to the marriage feast; and the door was shut. ¹¹Afterward the other maidens came also, saying, "Lord, lord, open to us." ¹²But he replied, "Truly, I say to you, I do not know you." ¹³Watch therefore, for you know neither the day nor the hour.

We Orthodox Christians believe that Christ will "come again in glory to judge the living and the dead," as we say each Sunday in the Creed during the Divine Liturgy. What does that mean for you and me, average Orthodox Christians? Part of the answer comes from the Parable of the Ten Maidens which Jesus told shortly before His Trial, Crucifixion, and Resurrection.

A Village Wedding: Model For the Second Coming

"Then the kingdom of heaven shall be compared to ten maidens who took their lamps and went to meet the bridegroom."

In this parable Jesus used the traditional customs of marriages in the villages of His time as a model for His teaching on preparing for His Second Coming. In order to understand the parable we need to look at these customs. On the day of the wedding, the groom would go to the house of the bride. There he would meet with the father of the bride and sign dowry agreements. It was not a religious service, but a social, legal, and financial arrangement.

Then around sundown, the entire wedding party would return to the home of the groom to celebrate the marriage. So that they would not return to a darkened home, it was the custom for young women, usually friends of the bride, to stand in front of the groom's house to welcome the bridal party with lighted oil lamps as they approached for the festivities.

Two Ways to Wait

"Five of them were foolish and five were wise. For when the foolish took their lamps, they took no oil with them; but the wise took flasks of oil with their lamps."

This is the main point of the story. Some of the young women prepared properly; some did not. The five wise maidens knew that the groom and the bridal party might be delayed, so they brought extra oil. The patristic commentators interpret the extra oil primarily as being prepared. But they also describe this preparation as consisting of two elements. St. John Chrysostom talks about good deeds, and especially about works of philanthropy and caring for the poor and the suffering.

Other Orthodox commentators, while not ignoring the philanthropic element, place the emphasis on the inner, spiritual life. True to the spirit of the Sermon on the Mount, they point to our inner dispositions of faith, commitment, unfeigned love for God and neighbor, humility, repentance, and genuine virtue.

Do you see what this parable teaches? Being prepared means cultivating your Christian life, both in your inner dispositions and in your deeds, so you recognize and are recognized by the Lord upon His return at the Second Coming.

If You're Not Ready When He Comes It's Too Late for You

"But at midnight there was a cry, 'Behold, the bridegroom! Come out to meet him.'"

In the Bible, midnight, the darkest hour, represents the suddenness and the unexpectedness of the Day of the Lord. No one knows when Christ will return. Those foolish Christians who scour the Scriptures for hints of a supposed physical and historical battle of Armageddon or craftily divide the biblical history into numerous so-called dispensations, and predict disjointed biblical passages on the basis of the most flimsy interpretations of the date of Christ's return are all wrong. When they do these things they disobey Christ, for Jesus specifically taught: "But of that day and hour no one knows, not even the angels of heaven, nor the Son, but the Father only" (Matt. 24:36). The point of this parable is to tell the real truth: we are always to be ready to meet the Lord.

"And the foolish said to the wise, 'Give us some of your oil, for our lamps are going out.' But the wise replied, 'Perhaps there will not be enough for us and for you; go rather to the dealers and buy for yourselves.'"

The wise maidens are not cruel or mean. For the purpose of the story is to teach us that last minute solutions cannot save us in the Judgment Day if we have not been living the way God wants us to live. When Christ comes, whenever that may be, we must be ready. We can't expect others to do for us what we alone must do for ourselves. We cannot make the prayers of others our own. We cannot take credit for the philanthropy of others. The faith of our neighbors cannot be credited to us. Neither can their love, their obedience, their service, or their repentance. In short, we must all do our own preparing for the Last Judgment.

In this parable Jesus is telling us that whether the end comes when we die or when He returns to judge the living and the dead, each of us is responsible to be ready. If we are ready, we will be numbered among the faithful, and the wise. Lukewarm, nominal Christianity will do us no good on that day, and it will be too late then to do anything about it. The time for preparing is now!

Serious Consequences

"...and those who were ready went in with him to the marriage feast."

The five maidens who had brought extra oil with them were prepared when the wedding party was delayed. They were ready with an emergency supply of oil. So also are those Christians who live their lives daily in faith and obedience to God, whose hearts and spirits turn toward Him in love and devotion, and whose deeds reflect that faith and love. So, when they meet the Lord, either at their death or at His Second Coming, He will recognize them and welcome them into His eternal Kingdom. But those whose lives are unprepared have another end.

"Afterward the other maidens came also, saying, 'Lord, Lord, open to us.' But he replied, 'Truly, I say to you, I do not know you.'"

"I do not know you!" What fearsome words for a Christian to hear! If we are like those foolish maidens, Jesus says He doesn't know us. Why?

* Because we never talk to Him in prayer.
* Because we don't do good deeds in His name.
* Because we don't long for His presence.
* Because we rarely struggle over what it means to serve Him.
* Because we hardly ever sacrifice for Him.

For these reasons we will not be ready to meet Him as persons whom He knows when He comes again. How sad and tragic for a person who bears the name Christian to hear Christ say to him *"I do not know you..."*

Shaking Up Nominal Christians

The parable ends with words designed to shake up nominal Christians and to alert us to what we must do. Nominal Christians are Christians mostly in name only. The words are serious and fateful. *"Watch, therefore, for you know neither the day nor the hour."*

Be ready, He says. Be ready every day. Be ready every hour. Be ready every minute.

* Watch.
* Be ready.
* For you know neither the day nor the hour.

The Sixth Epistle – Reflection 1

The Works of the Flesh – What a Christian Life Is Not Like
Galatians 5:22-6:3

> [22]*But the fruit of the Spirit is love, joy, peace, patience, kindness, goodness, faithfulness,* [23]*gentleness, self-control; against such there is no law.* [24]*And those who belong to Christ Jesus have crucified the flesh with its passions and desires.* [25]*If we live by the Spirit, let us also walk by the Spirit.* [26]*Let us have no self-conceit, no provoking of one another, no envy of one another.* [1]*Brethren, if a man is overtaken in any trespass, you who are spiritual should restore him in a spirit of gentleness. Look to yourself, lest you too be tempted.* [2]*Bear one another's burdens, and so fulfil the law of Christ.* [3]*For if any one thinks he is something, when he is nothing, he deceives himself.*

What is a real, genuine Christian life like? That's a difficult question to answer fully or completely, because the circumstances of our lives are so varied and changing. Each situation requires a Christian to act in Godlike ways that are fitting and appropriate to a follower of Christ. Rules can be guides, give directions, and set limits, but real life cannot be captured in a formula.

Nevertheless, the Bible does give a broad and general description of what a Christian life should be like and what it is not like. We find one of those descriptions (among several in the New Testament) in St. Paul's letter to the Christians of the Asia Minor province of Galatia.

Works of the Flesh

In the fifth chapter of this letter St. Paul gives us two lists of characteristics. One list consists of the works of the flesh. It gives a picture of a life that is not in harmony with God, not Godlike, not Christian. St. Paul described the life of the flesh like this: *"Now the works of the flesh are plain: fornication, impurity, licentiousness, idolatry, sorcery, enmity, strife, jealousy, anger, selfishness, dissension, party spirit, envy, drunkenness, carousing, and the like"* (Gal. 5:19-21).

From the last phrase (*"and the like"*) we understand that the list is not complete. But it does give us a general picture of a life that is out of kilter with the right use of our bodies (fornication, licentiousness, drunkenness, carousing), out of kilter with the right relationship with God (idolatry and sorcery), out of kilter with how we deal with other people (enmity, strife, dissension, jealousy, etc.), and our own inner mental and emotional being (envy, anger, selfishness).

"The Works of the Flesh" Understood Correctly

From the perspective of the Church, its Holy Tradition, and its reading of the Scriptures, the *works of the flesh* are not part of our human nature as God created us and wants us to be. They are the results of wrong choices on our part. It is true that repeated choices allowing us to succumb to the life of the flesh can become ingrained and sometimes even vicious habits. These habits can control us to the point that we feel our behaviors are somehow natural to us. However, they are really the most unnatural behaviors for people created in the image and likeness of God.

Many years ago, St. John Chrysostom opposed the view that our bodies themselves (flesh is understood as our physical existence), are the source of our sinfulness. Were he alive today, he would also oppose a similar argument made by those who say that their behavior is dictated by their genes. To people who think like this, Chrysostom wrote:

> Even if it be allowed that adultery and fornication proceed, as you assert, from the flesh; yet hatred, variance, emulations, strife, heresies, and witchcraft, these arise only from a depraved moral choice. And so it is with others also, for how can they belong to the flesh? You observe that he is not here speaking of the flesh, but of earthly thoughts, which trail upon the ground. Wherefore also he alarms them by saying, that "they who practice such things shall not inherit the kingdom of God." If these things belonged to nature and not to a bad moral choice, his expression, "they practice," is inappropriate; it should be, "they suffer." And why should they be cast out of the kingdom, for rewards and punishments relate not to what proceeds from nature but from choice.

With these words, Chrysostom points to the responsibility we have for our moral behavior. He clearly expressed the Orthodox Church's perspective when he added ". . . the mastery of the passions (meaning sinful desires and behaviors, not emotions or feelings) belongs to the soul, and concerns the soul. And being placed between vice and virtue, if the soul has used the body fitly, it has crafted it to be spiritual; but if the soul separate from the (Holy) Spirit and give itself up to evil desires, it makes itself more earthly."

Making Choices

Our behaviors, both good and bad, are certainly influenced by our physical and bodily existence (yes, even our genes). But what we do with these influences is up to us. To say that our behavior is determined by our bodies in some instinctual way, implies that we no longer have anything divine-like in us. You see, in that case, we would be minimally different from animals as far as morality is concerned. Commenting on this passage,

Chrysostom added, "You observe throughout that St. Paul's discourse does not relate to the substance of the flesh, but to the moral choice, which is or is not vicious."

Some might accept the view that bodily desires determine behaviors, but Orthodox Christians cannot. Our behaviour is determined by the moral and spiritual choices we make. Our goal as Christians is to reflect Godlikeness in our lives. It is clear that *"the works of the flesh"* do not characterize a God-like life. It is up to us to decide and to act in ways that will consistently avoid the works of the flesh.

The Fruit of the Spirit

Later in the same chapter, St. Paul tells the Galatian Christians (and us) about the Godlike characteristic that come to us as a result of communion with God in Jesus Christ and the Holy Spirit. This list characterizes the life that is lived in the Spirit: *"But the fruit of the Spirit is love, joy, peace, patience, kindness, goodness, faithfulness, gentleness, self-control"* (Gal. 5:22-23).

Of course, this also is not a complete list. But it does give us a picture of the way the Christian life is lived. Before looking at these nine characteristics in the following reflection, we need to understand something distinctive about the fruit of the Spirit.

St. Paul began the description of the behaviors and attitudes that do characterize the Christian life with the words, *"But the fruit of the Spirit is. . . ."* It is interesting to compare this to the behaviors and attitudes that are not Christian. They are *"works of the flesh"* (plural) but the *"fruit of the Spirit"* is singular. St. John Chrysostom, commenting on this difference wrote, ". . . it is because evil works originate in ourselves alone, and therefore he calls them 'works,' but good works require not only our diligence but God's loving kindness. He places first the root of these good things (in the Spirit of God), and then proceeds to recount them . . . ."

In other words, we do not live the Christian life exclusively through our own efforts. The living presence of God in our lives is a result of His outreaching love for us through Jesus Christ and in the Holy Spirit. The presence of God in our lives is the root from which the Christian life grows. We must be grafted into God to live the Christian life (Rom. 11:17-24).

Synergy

As we've seen, Chrysostom also pointed out that this doesn't mean the Christian life comes automatically, without effort on our part. The soul's choosing power is critical. Fitting and right choices can make even the body spiritual. Note what Chrysostom said, "if the soul separate from the (Holy) Spirit and give itself up to evil desires, it makes itself more earthly." In Orthodox theology and instruction regarding the spiritual and ethical life, this is called *synergy*. Synergy occurs when the human being willingly cooperates with the leading of God to avoid *the works of the flesh* and to be a suitable vineyard for the *fruit of the Spirit*. The Spirit of God produces the fruit in us. It is up to us to keep ourselves cultivated and fertile to grow the fruit of the Spirit.

What Happens to a Spiritual Vacuum?

Do you see what this means? The works of the flesh take over when we offer no synergy for God's Spirit to work in us. A condition which might be called a spiritual vacuum is created when we are separated from God's presence and He is not present in our lives. The vacuum doesn't last long, however. It is quickly filled with the corrupting and demonic presence of evil.

Even if we manage to get rid of bad and perverse habits for a time on our own, if the space vacated by them is not filled with the presence of the One in whose image we have been created, the works of the flesh return and take up their residence in us again. Jesus once described this process dramatically:

> When the unclean spirit has gone out of a man,
> he passes through waterless places seeking rest;
> and finding none he says, "I will return to my house
> from which I came." And when he comes he finds
> it swept and put in order. Then he goes and brings
> seven other spirits more evil than himself, and they

> *enter and dwell there; and the last state of that man becomes worse than the first (Lk. 11:24-26).*

The result is predictable. We become addicted to the works of the flesh: *"Now the works of the flesh are plain: fornication, impurity, licentiousness, idolatry, sorcery, enmity, strife, jealousy, anger, selfishness, dissension, party spirit, envy, drunkenness, carousing, and the like"* (Gal. 5:19-21).

The Sixth Epistle – Reflection 2

The Fruit of the Spirit – What a Christian Life Is Like
Galatians 5:22-6:3

> ^{22}But the fruit of the Spirit is love, joy, peace, patience, kindness, goodness, faithfulness, ^{23}gentleness, self-control; against such there is no law. ^{24}And those who belong to Christ Jesus have crucified the flesh with its passions and desires. ^{25}If we live by the Spirit, let us also walk by the Spirit. ^{26}Let us have no self-conceit, no provoking of one another, no envy of one another. ^{1}Brethren, if a man is overtaken in any trespass, you who are spiritual should restore him in a spirit of gentleness. Look to yourself, lest you too be tempted. ^{2}Bear one another's burdens, and so fulfil the law of Christ. ^{3}For if any one thinks he is something, when he is nothing, he deceives himself.

As you read this passage do you sense a paradox in it? On the one hand, *"the fruit of the Spirit"* is a list of character traits that are described as coming to us from the Spirit of God. The fruit of the Spirit is a gift to us from Jesus Christ through the Holy Spirit. That's why there can be no law or rules regarding the fruit of the Spirit, it is beyond our control since it is a gift from God.

Yet, at the same time, we are responsible for setting up part of the conditions that make space in our lives for the fruit of the Spirit. For you see, *"those who belong to Christ Jesus have crucified the flesh with its passions and desires."* We are told, *"If we live by the Spirit, let us also walk by the Spirit."* So, somehow, we too are involved and responsible for experiencing the fruit of the Spirit in our lives.

It would seem that these two aspects of the Christian life walk hand in hand: the Christian life is both a gift from God and the result of our following the way of the Lord by choice, decision, and action. The two are interconnected. The grace of God is in the lead for our growth in the Christian life. But we must cooperate with it freely and energetically.

Fruit of the Spirit / Gifts of the Spirit

In the preceding reflection we noted together with St. John Chrysostom that while the results of our sinful choices were described in the plural as *works* of the flesh, the result of the activity of the Holy Spirit in our lives is described in the singular, *fruit* of the Spirit. The reason is, of course, that the Spirit of God is the *one* source of all spiritual graces.

Elsewhere in the New Testament we read of *gifts*. These gifts are different from the *fruit of the Holy Spirit*. Spiritual *gifts* are given personally to each Christian for the purpose of building up others in the Church. They are unique and special personal ways of service. In the letter to the Romans, for example, St. Paul wrote that we individually have *"gifts that differ according to the grace given to us"* (Rom. 12:6).

But the fruit of the Spirit is common to all Christians who live the life in God. We will look at the various aspects of the *fruit of the Spirit* in this and the next reflection, and will come to more deeply understand what the genuine Christian life ought to be for all of us. The fruit of the Spirit in us consists of the Godlike characteristics, attitudes, and ways of relating that fit the life of a person growing in God's image and likeness.

The Result of Growth in the Spirit

Growth in the Spirit of God, brings spiritual fruit to all of us. These spiritual characteristics come to us in the measure that our hearts, minds, and spirits receive them and make for them a hospitable environment in the way we think, speak, act, worship, and pray.

What comes from these spiritual characteristics is a unified Godlike way of being a follower of the Lord and a member of His body, the Church.

Love

Let's look at St. Paul's list of these characteristics of the Christlike life briefly. He begins with *love*. Zigabenos, a late Byzantine biblical commentator, summarizes the importance of love as a starting point. He writes, "He placed love first as the most inclusive of all these good things, their root and their cause." The Orthodox Christian tradition teaches two basic things about love. Love in our lives is based on God's love, and God's love has two sides to it. We first learn about God's love in His selfless care and concern for our well-being. *"We love, because God first loved us"* (1 John 4:19). God shows His love for us through the creation, making us like Him, sending His Son Jesus Christ to heal and redeem us through His death on the Cross and His Resurrection, and through sending us His sustaining and sanctifying Holy Spirit in His Church.

All of this we duplicate in our lives when we act for our neighbor's well-being, motivated primarily by concern for our neighbor's good. When we act that way toward others we express God's love to others.

We have also learned that God is a Trinity of divine persons — Father, Son, and Holy Spirit — who live in unity, harmony, and mutual communion with each other: the one God. Christian love begins with selfless service for the other, but it ends in communion, unity, and harmony with God and among people. In this way, human love reflects the love of the Holy Trinity. The first fruit of the Spirit that characterizes the Christian life is this twofold kind of love. It is the source and fountain of all the other dimensions of the Holy Spirit in the Christian's life.

Joy

St. Paul follows love with *joy*. The Christian also receives his joy and happiness from God. Jesus said to His disciples *"These things I have spoken to you, that my joy might be in you, and that your joy may be full"* (Jn. 15:11). The joy that we talk about here is not fun, or good times, in the way the world experiences them. Not that fun and good times are in themselves always bad. The joy of the Spirit springs from a deep confidence that we are eternally supported by the loving arms of God. This joy remains, even in adversity, difficulty, and pain. "Rejoice" was one of the first greetings that Christians used to greet each other.

Being a Christian is a happy thing because in the love of God, we know and experience where we fit in the scheme of things. We are not anxious, because we trust in God and His providential care for us. St. Paul wrote, *"We know that in everything God works for good with those who love him, who are called according to his purpose"* (Rom. 8:28). The second fruit of the Spirit, joy, comes to us not by our own doing, but as a result of the presence of the Spirit of God in our lives. Since that presence cannot exist without love, we see that joy and love are inevitably interconnected.

Peace

The third fruit of the Spirit is *peace*. Jesus granted peace to His disciples. St. John Chrysostom, in his thirty-second homily on the Gospel of Matthew indicates that "This peace Christ also declared to be great, when He said, 'Peace I leave with you, my peace I give unto you' (Jn. 14:27). And we should do all things, so as to enjoy it, both at home and in church."

Peace is a fruit of the Holy Spirit; yet, we must act to make ourselves open to it. We need to be hospitable environments for the peace of God to penetrate us as a fruit of the Holy Spirit. Otherwise, as Chrysostom said, we can alienate it according to our "disposition," for "this peace both comes and flies away again. . .

on the worthiness of them that receive." And, in the same place, Chrysostom cautions us, "Neither let us account it a small loss, not to enjoy such peace." In an age of excessive activity, conflict, and violence, it *is* a great loss if we fail to make space for this fruit of the Spirit in our lives.

One way we can prepare our souls for the peace of God is by cultivating love and joy in our hearts. Another way is to be Godlike in becoming, where we can, a peacemaker by cultivating a peaceful relationship with God through Jesus Christ in the Spirit, and then reaching out to others in peace. In the New Testament we are told how peace and a close relationship with God are intimately connected. *"Strive for peace with all men, and for the holiness without which no one will see the Lord"* (Heb. 12:14).

In commenting on the verse in Matthew 5:9, Chrysostom reminds us of a further dimension of peace: *"'Blessed are the peace-makers.'* Here He not only takes away altogether our own strife and hatred in ourselves, but He requires besides this something more, namely, that we should bring together in unity other, who are at strife."

The circle comes around fully from the peace we seek to bring to human relations to the peace we need to have from God. In reflecting on the passage in 1 Peter 3:11 Chrysostom wrote: *"'Seek peace, and pursue it.'* I mean not peace with man only, but also peace with God."

We need love and joy and peace, and all three come together from God.

The Sixth Epistle – Reflection 3

The Fruit of the Spirit – Continued
Galatians 5:22-6:3

[22]But the fruit of the Spirit is love, joy, peace, patience, kindness, goodness, faithfulness, [23]gentleness, self-control; against such there is no law. [24]And those who belong to Christ Jesus have crucified the flesh with its passions and desires. [25]If we live by the Spirit, let us also walk by the Spirit. [26]Let us have no self-conceit, no provoking of one another, no envy of one another. [1]Brethren, if a man is overtaken in any trespass, you who are spiritual should restore him in a spirit of gentleness. Look to yourself, lest you too be tempted. [2]Bear one another's burdens, and so fulfil the law of Christ. [3]For if any one thinks he is something, when he is nothing, he deceives himself.

The six remaining aspects of the fruit of the Spirit are patience, kindness, goodness, faithfulness, gentleness, and self-control. In this reflection we will explore what these mean for committed Orthodox Christian believers seeking to live the life in Christ.

Patience

The great fourth century church father, St. Gregory the Theologian, spoke lovingly of his sister Gorgonia at her funeral. A devoted and faithful Christian, Gorgonia had suffered much in her life. St. Gregory praised her patience and God's loving kindness toward her. "Although her suffering was human, her recovery was superhuman, and she gave to posterity a compelling argument for the display of faith in affliction and patient endurance in misfortune, but a far greater one for the loving kindness of God toward such as she."

Like Gorgonia, we Christians who are seeking to live in a Godlike way, will be called at one time or another to make "a display of faith in affliction and patient endurance in misfortune," and thus show the committedness of our whole life to Christ, our God. But in this exercise of patient endurance we will also show how God works in us and in our lives. We will concurrently be revealing "the loving kindness of God toward" us.

What connects those two expressions of patience? It is interesting to see in just one letter of St. Paul, how our efforts toward patience in Christian living and the grace of patience as a fruit of the Holy Spirit in our lives are connected.

In the letter to the Colossian Christians, St. Paul begins by praying that they may receive from God the blessing of patience. He says, *"May you be strengthened with all power, according to his glorious might, for all endurance and patience with joy, giving thanks to the Father, who has qualified us to share in the inheritance of the saints in light"* (Col. 1:11-12). Later, in the same letter, St. Paul instructs the Colossian Christians to assume the responsibility themselves to *"put on then, as God's chosen ones, holy and beloved, compassion, kindness, lowliness, meekness, and patience, forbearing one another . . ."* (Col. 3:13).

In the first case, God is called upon to help us endure painful circumstances. In the second, we are called upon ourselves *"to put on . . . patience"* among other virtues. Why should we deal with difficult circumstances and irritating people with patience?

St. Paul gives us reasons in both these cases. In the first case, it is because Christ is our Savior who came as the Son of God and took on human nature, taught us, healed us, died for us on the Cross, and conquered the forces of death, sin and evil and with His Resurrection. In verses 13 and 14 of chapter 1, St. Paul gives the reason for his prayer: *"He (Christ) has delivered us from the dominion of darkness and transferred us to the kingdom of his beloved Son, in whom we have redemption, the forgiveness of sins."* So you see, the source of every virtue, including patience, is the redeeming work of Jesus Christ.

In the second case, we are called as Christians to be patient in circumstances and with people precisely because Christians are supposed to be imitators of God, seeking to live Godlike lives. So in Colossians 3:13-14, immediately following the passage that reads *"put on . . . patience,"* St. Paul instructs us, *". . . and, if one has a complaint against another, forgiving each other; as the Lord has forgiven you, so you also must forgive."*

Patience is possible because Christ is our Savior. We ought to be patient, because as Christians, we are supposed to be Godlike.

Kindness

The fruit of the Spirit translated as *kindness* is an effort to put into English the Greek word, *chrestotes*. This word describes the condition of being *chrestos. Chrestos* means worthy or good so it is only a little different from goodness. A modern Orthodox commentator made the following comments about this aspect of the fruit of the Spirit: "Because 'goodness' follows, it rather means a benevolent disposition and the willingness to do good to others. Also, worthy of consideration is the view that it refers to graciousness in relationships and being approachable, especially to those dependent upon us . . . as well as polite and open, even to those who have harmed us."

Goodness

Following so closely upon *kindness*, which is understood more as the internal disposition toward goodness, *goodness* itself means that the Spirit produces in us a habitual inclination to do good to others in actions, especially to those in need.

This too comes from God, who according to the Church Fathers, is the source of goodness itself. St. Augustine, in his commentary on Psalm 134 observes: "How good is that good from which all goods are derived! No good whatsoever can be discovered whose goodness is not derived from that good. That good which makes things good is truly good." That is why, when you and I as faithful and believing Christians do good things to others, we praise God. We know that ultimately, the good we do is part of the fruit of the Spirit.

Faithfulness

The Greek word translated here as *faithfulness* is *pistis*. This word has provoked some discussion. The translation understands the Greek word to mean something like trustworthiness, that is, to be a person to whom it has been given to be depended upon to do what he or she is required to do.

Another interpretation understands *pistis* as being given strong and powerful faith. Early in the history of the Church, the biblical commentator Origen (185-254) connected *pistis* with the *faith that can move mountains* (Matt. 17:20).

Others hold that *pistis* is used here to mean a person who is a worthy witness, who tells the truth, who is not a liar.

What St. Paul had in mind when he used the word *"pistis"* as a characteristic of the fruit of the Spirit is not absolutely clear to us. But it might be safe to say that all three of these understandings certainly fit everything else that we know about the Godlike life. If you are an Orthodox Christian in whom the fruit of the Spirit resides, you will be trustworthy and dependable in your duties and responsibilities (Rom. 3:3; Tit. 2:10); you will believe deeply in God and His energies in your life (Mk. 11:23); and, you will be a truthful and honest person, whose "yes" will be "yes," and whose "no" will be "no" (Matt. 5:27).

Gentleness

The Greek word translated here as *gentleness* is *praotes*. In the writings of the Church Fathers the opposites of gentleness are described as "anger" (St. Gregory of Nyssa, *On the Beatitudes*), "rage" (St. John Chrysostom, *On Acts*) and "indolence," meaning being uninvolved and unconcerned (St. Basil, *Ascetic Rule*). You will remember Jesus' words at the beginning of the Sermon on the

Mount: "Blessed are the meek (*praeis*), for they shall inherit the earth" (Matt. 5:5). That beatitude could also read: "Blessed are the gentle, for they shall inherit the earth."

In any case, many Christians have had trouble with this passage. In an activist society like ours, it carries the implication that being retiring, wishy-washy, passive, and uninvolved is blessed. But, if St. Basil is right, indolence, uninvolvement, and lack of concern are the opposite of gentleness.

How is gentleness to be understood then, both as a characteristic of the fruit of the Spirit and our own chosen way of behaving? St. Gregory of Nyssa provides an important definition of *praotes* (gentleness) in his book *On the Beatitudes*. He wrote, "This, then, is gentleness: to develop resistance and to slowly learn to oppose the drives of our (fallen) nature." Far from being weakness, if we are gentle persons, we are attentive to what provokes us to anger and rage. If you are a gentle person you learn not to respond to provocations produced by others and on their terms. If you are gentle, you determine the circumstances and conditions of every encounter. Gentleness makes it possible for you to take charge of the many difficult and unpleasant situations you may face.

Now, think what this has to say to another puzzling and sometimes hard to understand passage from the New Testament. *"You have heard that it was said, 'An eye for an eye and a tooth for a tooth.' But I say to you, Do not resist one who is evil"* (Matt. 5:38-39).

Self-Control

This understanding of gentleness leads effortlessly to *self-control*. While gentleness focuses on your relationships with others (not allowing others to provoke your anger, but by gentleness taking control of the situation), self-control focuses on you, your inner dispositions and your mental and spiritual state. The Greek word translated here as self-control is *engrateia*. So, you understand now why St. Maximos the Confessor (580-662) said in his *Fourth Century on Love* that "A soul's motivation is rightly ordered when its desiring power is subordinated to self-control . . ." A monk by the name of Thalassios gives us this advice: "If you wish to be in control of your soul and body, forestall the passions (sins) by rooting out their causes. Yoke the powers of the soul to the virtues and they will be freed from the tyranny of the passions. Curb the impulses of desire by means of self-control and those of anger with spiritual love."

Fruit and Effort

The fruit of the Spirit is an interconnected and inter-related web of Godlike living. Each trait of the Christian life comes to us from God through the Holy Spirit. Baptized and chrismated with the "seal of the gift of the Holy Spirit," we are recipients of love, joy, peace, patience, kindness, faithfulness, gentleness, and self-control. It is up to us to cultivate them in communion with God, so that we can reflect that communion in our choices, determining and acting as followers of God the Father through the salvation we have received in Christ, living in and with the Holy Spirit.

The Sixth Gospel

Faithful Persistence
Matthew 15:21-28

²¹*And Jesus went away from there and withdrew to the district of Tyre and Sidon.* ²²*And behold, a Canaanite woman from that region came out and cried, "Have mercy on me, O Lord, Son of David; my daughter is severely possessed by a demon."* ²³*But he did not answer her a word. And his disciples came and begged him, saying, "Send her away, for she is crying after us."* ²⁴*He answered, "I was sent only to the lost sheep of the house of Israel."* ²⁵*But she came and knelt before him, saying, "Lord, help me."* ²⁶*And he answered, "It is not fair to take the children's bread and throw it to the dogs."* ²⁷*She said, "Yes, Lord, yet even the dogs eat the crumbs that fall from their masters' table."* ²⁸*Then Jesus answered her, "O woman, great is your faith! Be it done for you as you desire." And her daughter was healed instantly.*

This passage has created difficulty for some contemporary animal-loving Christians. It also raises questions about Christ's relationship with this non-Jewish woman. It seems out of character for Jesus to treat her so meanly. Just exactly what was happening in this encounter? Is there a message in it for us?

Dogs

Let's deal with the dog question right away. There is no question that Jesus' response was intended to put the lady down.

You see, in the ancient world dogs were thought of less as pets and more as scavengers. Homer decried dogs eating the corpses of fallen soldiers as a horrible fate. The Bible reflects this ancient attitude. For example, the prophet Elijah threatened the evil king Ahab, who unjustly killed Naboth to get his vineyard. *"In the place where dogs licked up the blood of Naboth shall dogs lick your own blood"* (1 Kings 21:19). To call a person a dog in the ancient world was, indeed, an insult.

When dogs no longer had to find their own food, and became household pets, oftentimes quite pampered and always well-fed, our attitudes about them changed because their behavior changed. From the time of Shakespeare literature abounds with positive references about dogs. An American senator in 1884 summed up these attitudes when he said in a speech, "The one absolutely unselfish friend that man can have in this selfish world, the one that never deserts him, the one that never proves ungrateful or treacherous, is a dog. When all other friends desert, he remains."

Three Rebuffs

So, one day this woman from another national group (Matthew calls her a Canaanite woman and Mark in chapter 7:26, identifies her as "a Greek, a Syrophoenician by birth") asked Jesus to heal her sick daughter. She made her request reverently and respectfully: *"Have mercy on me, O Lord, Son of David."* She clearly believed that Jesus had the power to heal her daughter, so she was both reverent and believing.

Jesus responded by rebuffing her three times. First, He didn't answer her, as if He had not heard her. Secondly, when the disciples tire of her appeals, they asked Jesus to *"Send her away, for she is crying after us."* But, with the woman in earshot, Christ seemed to eliminate her from those whom He cared about: *"I was sent only to the lost sheep of the house of Israel."* Thirdly, He used an ethical argument to refuse her request: *"It is not fair to take the children's bread and throw it to the dogs."*

This response is so unlike the Jesus we know from the rest of the gospels! How can we understand this "out of character" episode in the life of our loving, compassionate, and caring Lord?

Faithful Persistence

In his sermon "On Lowliness of Mind," St. John Chrysostom does not soften Christ's treatment of the woman. He does not even apologize for Jesus comparing her to the lowly dogs. He does not minimize her foreign nationality. In fact, Chrysostom goes to substantial lengths to show that this Canaanite woman was somehow unworthy.

Yet, Chrysostom opens up to us the mind-process of Christ in regard to this woman so as to show us what was happening in this episode, and even more importantly, what real and deep lessons there are for us to follow. Here is what this great Church Father understands to be taking place in this story.

> At the beginning and in the prelude of her request He answered nothing; but when both once and twice and thrice she had come to him, then He granted the blessing. By the conclusion of the episode, He convinces us that He had delayed the giving, not that He might repel her but that He might display to us all the woman's endurance. For if He had delayed in order that He might repel her, He would not have granted it even at the end. But since He was waiting to display to all her spiritual wisdom, on this account He was silent. For if He had granted it immediately and at the beginning, we should not have known the woman's virtue. "Let her go" it says, "because she is clamoring behind us." But what (says) the Christ? "You hear a voice, but I see the mind: I know what she is going to say. I choose not to permit the treasure hidden in her mind to escape notice; but I am waiting and keeping silence; in order that having

discovered it I may lay it down in publicity, and make it manifest to all."

So, Chrysostom said that Jesus' response was the way by which the woman's inner world was more persistently and intensely externalized! By appearing to be aloof from her appeals, Christ made clear and unmistakable this foreign woman's endurance, her virtue and her spiritual wisdom. Not only did the quality of her inner life become clear to the disciples and the other onlookers, but in the end, Jesus praises her for her great faith. What appears to be disinterest and lack of concern on Jesus' part, is, in fact, a way of showing love, not only for the Greek Syrophoenician woman, but also for His disciples and all those who follow *the Way*.

Assiduity

What precisely was the Canaanite woman's inner spiritual virtue that Jesus wanted to reveal so that she would be blessed with the healing of her daughter and so that the disciples (and we) could profit spiritually? In his explanation, St. John Chrysostom uses the word "assiduity" in the translation. This older English word is a characteristic of a person who is diligent, energetic, industrious, persevering, persistent, resolute, and zealous. No wonder Jesus said to her *"O woman, great is your faith! Be it done for you as you desire"*!

Chrysostom explains: "Never mind," he says, "that you are unworthy. Become worthy by your assiduity. For it is possible both that the unworthy should become worthy from his assiduity, and that God assents more when called on by ourselves than by others."

Lesson One: Persistence in Prayer

The first lesson Chrysostom drew from the example of the Canaanite woman is based on her persistence in appealing to Christ for the healing of her daughter. One tradition of continuous prayer, based on the New Testament injunction, *"Pray unceasingly"* (1 Thess. 5:17) is the practice of the Jesus Prayer. By continuously repeating the prayer "Lord Jesus Christ, Son of God, have mercy on me, a sinner" the Orthodox monastic tradition has taught the Church a method for perpetual prayer that is worthy of emulation. We will discuss this further in the next reflection. Here, Saint John Chrysostom teaches us another way to unceasing prayer.

> We (should) always resort to prayers as a refuge, and pray to the God who gives the word of wisdom to grant both intelligence in hearing, and a careful and unconquerable guardianship of this spiritual deposit in our hands. For things which often we have not strength to perform successfully from our own exertions, these we shall have power to accomplish easily through prayers. I mean prayers which are persevering. For always and without intermission it is a duty to pray.

God might respond immediately to our prayerful petitions, Chrysostom argues, precisely so that we will stay close to Him. Staying close to Him is exactly what human beings are supposed to do to be real and true human beings, growing in His image and likeness toward Godlikeness. It is no more and no less than what a good parent does. It is, says Chrysostom "just in the way also that affectionate fathers do; for they also adroitly manage the perpetual and assiduous attendance of children who are rather indolent by the delay of the giving."

Lesson Two: Personal Prayer

Secondly, Chrysostom pointed to the personal character of the Canaanite woman's prayer. Clearly, Chrysostom did not reject intercessory prayer, that is, praying for others or asking others to pray for us. Since the Church in heaven and the Church on earth are one, we can and should ask for intercessory prayers. We can ask our priest, family members, people in our parish, monks, nuns, saints, and angels to pray for us.

But intercessary prayer is not a substitute for our own prayers. On that Chrysostom is adamant. While you *can and should ask* for the intercessions of others, you *must* also pray yourself. This is how Chrysostom puts it:

> Even if we be in sins, and unworthy of receiving, let us not despair; knowing, that by assiduity of soul we shall be able to become worthy of the request. Even if we be unaided by advocate and destitute, let us not faint; knowing that it is a strong advocacy, the coming to God one's self by one's self with much eagerness.

Lesson Three: Sinners, Pray!

Sometimes we feel ashamed to pray. We do things we should not do. We do not do things we should do. How can we stand before God and try to speak to Him when we are so bad? Chrysostom knew about this feeling of unworthiness, and he interpreted this passage in his twenty-second homily on Matthew precisely by putting the sinner in the shoes of the Canaanite woman. He said, "Let us therefore draw close to Him, and say, 'In truth, Lord, even the dogs eat of the crumbs which fall from their masters' table.'"

But he added significantly, "Let us draw close 'in season, out of season'; or rather, one can never draw close to God out of season, for it is unseasonable not to be continually approaching Him."

The Seventh Epistle

Christian Freedom
2 Thessalonians 5:14-24

[14]And we exhort you, brethren, admonish the idlers, encourage the fainthearted, help the weak, be patient with them all. [15]See that none of you repays evil for evil, but always seek to do good to one another and to all. [16]Rejoice always, [17]pray constantly, [18]give thanks in all circumstances; for this is the will of God in Christ Jesus for you. [19]Do not quench the Spirit, [20]do not despise prophesying, [21]but test everything; hold fast what is good, [22]abstain from every form of evil. [23]May the God of peace himself sanctify you wholly; and may your spirit and soul and body be kept sound and blameless at the coming of our Lord Jesus Christ. [24]He who calls you is faithful, and he will do it.

Many scholars think that the first epistle to the Christians in the Greek city of Thessalonica on the northeastern shore of the Mediterranean Sea was the first writing of our New Testament. The church in Thessalonica was established by St. Paul in the summer 50 A.D.

The letter was written about a year later to address some problems that had arisen in the newly-established church. This letter set a pattern for most of the letters in the New Testament. The earlier parts of these letters generally deal with issues of faith, belief, or general themes. The latter part of the letters have a practical character.

The passage we have before us comes from the latter part of this letter. Beyond being instructional, it is imperative, that is, it gives directions to the members of the new Christian community about how they are to live the Christian life. In this reflection we will look at just one aspect of this passage. We will see how these directions are expressed by St. Paul to the Christians of Thessalonica and what that means for the way we understand the living of the Christian life.

Being Exhorted to Christian Values

"And we exhort you, brethren, admonish the idlers, encourage the fainthearted, help the weak, be patient with them all."

What is most striking about this letter is that in each of the chapters, with the exception of the first (though twice in the fourth chapter), we find St. Paul using the word exhort as he speaks to the faithful of Thessalonica.

In chapter two, he exhorted them *"to lead a life worthy of God, who calls you into his own kingdom and glory"* (1 Thess. 2:12). In chapter three, the exhortation is that *"no one be moved by (certain) afflictions"* (1 Thess. 3:3). In chapter four, they are exhorted *"in the Lord Jesus, that as you learned from us how you ought to live and to please God, just as you are doing, you do so more and more"* (1 Thess. 4:1). And again in chapter four, St. Paul praised the Thessalonian Christians for their love, affirming that *"indeed you do love all the brethren throughout Macedonia. But we exhort you, brethren, to do so more and more . . ."* (1 Thess. 4:11). Finally, as we have seen above, he exhorts his fellow Christians in Thessalonica to *"admonish the idlers, encourage the fainthearted, help the weak, be patient with them all"* (1 Thess. 5:14).

St. Paul's Alternatives

It is important for Christians to understand the nature of St. Paul's exhortations. It is clear from this and other letters in the New Testament that there are expectations of the kinds of behaviors that either are or are not appropriate for Christians who are seeking to grow toward Godlikeness. There are things Christians *should* do; and there are things Christians *shouldn't* do. Christians need to know and understand these behavioral expectations and act accordingly.

The following behavioral expectations are covered in this passage:

* Christians should not be idle.
* Christians should be courageous and not fainthearted.
* Christians should be supportive of those who are weak and insecure.
* Christians should relate to all people with patience.
* Christians should be thankful in all circumstances.
* Christians should not quench the Spirit.

Throughout the Bible and the Holy Tradition of the Church, we find similar descriptions of right and wrong behavior.

The question we need to ask is this: Precisely how does St. Paul convey the message of right and wrong? What alternative modes of expression did he have? Well, if you think about it, you will see that St. Paul had several alternatives:

* He could have *demanded* that they behave like Christians on his personal authority.
* He could have *legalized* the instruction, that is, laid down the law with rules.
* He could have *threatened punishments*: "do this, *or else*."
* He could have sweetened his requirements with promises of *rewards*.

Though examples of all of these alternatives and more can be found in the Bible and in Holy Tradition, in this passage St. Paul uses a different approach.

Parakalo **and Exhort**

St. Paul *exhorts*, according to our translation. In every case in 1 Thessalonians, the Greek word which is translated as *exhort* is a form of the verb *parakalo*.

Modern Greeks often understand this word to mean "please," as in "Please bring me a glass of water." Sometimes in modern Greek it has the meaning of asking someone to act in a particular way. "I ask you (*"Se parakalo"*) to bring me a glass of water." In this sense it can be said gently, intensely, or even angrily. But in every case the implication of the word is that the person being asked is free to respond or not to respond.

In ancient and biblical Greek *parakalo* also has several distinct meanings. It can mean to call to, to beseech, to exhort, or to comfort. However, in the translation of First Thessalonians in the Revised Standard Version of the Bible, *parakalo* is always translated as exhort.

The English word exhort means, to urge earnestly; to admonish strongly (to do what is proper or required, or not to do something wrong or unfitting to the Christian life). In the case of both *parakalo* and exhort there is a calling to do what is right and ought to be done. Additionally, there is a sense of intensity in pointing to what should not be done.

But there seems to be a difference between *parakalo* and *exhort.* Exhort carries more of a sense of authority than *parakalo,* which carries more of a sense of brotherly imploring, of a friend who strongly appeals, pleads, and entreats an equal to behave in a way that is fitting and appropriate. *Parakalo* implores. Exhort has more of the feeling of imposing the desires of one person upon another.

Here, what ought to be done by these new Christians is not a legal demand. Nor is it an objective law or rule, nor a threat, nor a transaction promising a reward. It does not carry the feeling of imposition from the outside. It asks one to freely and willingly choose to conform to behavior that is fitting to the Christian life.

Doing God's Will Freely

Here is one of the greatest secrets of the Christian life! As we mature in the Christian life, we grow into doing what is right and avoiding what is wrong. The Christian life begins with rules, warnings of punishment, and promises of rewards, because we need such things to form us.

But living the Christian life eventually moves beyond such things. We are brought by God's grace to a point where we willingly and freely offer ourselves and our lives back to God as a gift to Him in response to His great love and mercy to us. Do you see how clear the logic is? *"In this the love of God was made manifest among us, that God sent his only Son into the world, so that we might live through him. In this is love, not that we loved God but that he loved us and sent his Son to be the expiation for our sins. Beloved, if God so loved us, we also ought to love one another"* (1 Jn. 4:9-11).

Another way of expressing the same truth can be found in a *parakalo* passage from St. Paul's letter to the Romans. In this verse, however, the translation reads *"I appeal,"* not, *"I exhort."* *"I appeal to you therefore, brethren, by the mercies of God, to present your bodies as a living sacrifice, holy and acceptable to God, which is your spiritual worship."*

Furthermore, *"Do not be conformed to this world but be transformed by the renewal of your mind, that you may prove what is the will of God, what is good and acceptable and perfect"* (Rom. 12:1-2).

Do you see what this means? If you are transformed and renewed in God through Christ and in the Holy Spirit, you no longer need to be commanded with rules; you no longer need to respond to threats; you no longer long after rewards. You live enough in communion with God so that your life conforms not with the world's values, but flows freely in harmony with God's way of living.

That is the definition of Christian freedom. It is not "I can do anything I want!" It is rather, "Since I belong to God, heart, soul, and body, I have no will to do anything but that which keeps me in communion with God, that is, *His* will!"

Words of True Freedom

* *"Now the Lord is the Spirit, and where the Spirit of the Lord is, there is freedom"* (2 Cor. 3:17).
* *"For freedom Christ has set us free; stand fast therefore, and do not submit again to a yoke of slavery"* (Gal. 5:1).

* *"For you were called to freedom, brethren; only do not use your freedom as an opportunity for the flesh, but through love be servants of one another"* (Gal. 5:13)
* *"Live as free men, yet without using your freedom as a pretext for evil, but live as servants of God"* (1 Pet. 2:16).
* *"Jesus then said to the Jews who had believed in him, 'If you continue in my word, you are truly my disciples, and you will know the truth, and the truth will make you free'"* (Jn. 8:31-32).

Yes! *"He who calls you is faithful, and he will do it!*

. . . May the God of peace himself sanctify you wholly; and may your spirit and soul and body be kept sound and blameless at the coming of our Lord Jesus Christ! (2 Thess. 5:24-25)

The Seventh Gospel

Marching Orders
Matthew 9:9-14

⁹As Jesus passed on from there, he saw a man called Matthew sitting at the tax office; and he said to him, "Follow Me." And he rose and followed him. ¹⁰And as he sat at table in the house, behold, many tax collectors and sinners came and sat down with Jesus and his disciples. ¹¹And when the Pharisees saw this, they said to his disciples, "Why does your teacher eat with tax collectors and sinners?" ¹²But when he heard it, he said, "Those who are well have no need of a physician, but those who are sick. ¹³Go and learn what this means, 'I desire mercy, and not sacrifice.' For I came not to call the righteous, but sinners."

The choice of this passage to conclude the readings for the healing Sacrament of Holy Unction is a profound one. As the final reading, it provides marching orders for us. We are called to action. Jesus was walking by the office of Matthew the tax collector. He stopped and turned to this man. We can imagine that their eyes met. Matthew no doubt had heard of Jesus in the town's gossip. Perhaps he had even seen Him before. Maybe there was a hidden longing inside him that saw in Jesus the potential for a new kind of life.

Whatever the case, that encounter changed Matthew's life. It initiated a series of events that can be a source of reflection for each of us. And those reflections can impel us, as well, to new steps that might prove just as revolutionary. You see, what we have in this gospel reading is a call to action: *"Follow Me,"* Jesus Christ says.

The Way of Choice

"As Jesus passed on from there, he saw a man called Matthew sitting at the tax office; and he said to him, 'Follow Me.' And he rose and followed him.""

St. John Chrysostom makes much of the exceptional transformation that took place with Matthew's immediate response to Christ's invitation in his commentary on this verse. Fishermen, he said, do something common and ordinary. Jesus said "Follow Me" to them, too. Out of decent and honest work Christ called Peter and Andrew to follow Him. And they did, leaving their nets (Mk. 1:16-17).

But the transition is not so radical as it was for Matthew. Everyone in the Jewish community agreed that being a tax collector was identical to being a sinner. The tax collectors worked on commission. The more taxes they collected from the Jews for the Romans, the more they could keep for themselves. Consequently, they cheated people; they extorted from both rich and poor.

But something was at work in Matthew. Chrysostom argues that Jesus knew to call Matthew precisely when he was ready in his soul to respond positively. So the immediate decision to follow Jesus was quite remarkable; it was a decision to obey Christ without hesitation. St. John Chrysostom says:

> But as you have seen the power of Him that called, so consider also the obedience of him that was called: how he neither resisted, nor disputing said, "What is this? Is this not indeed a deceitful calling, with which He calls me, being such as I am?" No! For this humility again would have had been out of season.
>
> Rather, he obeyed immediately, and did not even request to go home, and to communicate with his relations concerning this matter . . . . (He) followed, exhibiting a mind prepared for all things; and breaking

himself at once away from all worldly things, by his complete obedience he bore witness that He who called him had chosen a good time.

Contrast this with the rich young man who heard the words *"Follow Me!"* from Jesus, but rejected the invitation. Jesus said to him, *"You lack one thing; go, sell what you have, and give to the poor, and you will have treasure in heaven; and come, follow me"* (Mk. 10:21). But he turned away. Both Matthew and the rich young man were free to respond. One responded positively and became a devoted disciple. The other walked away sadly.

Similarly, we too, have a choice. The invitation is extended to all of us. *"Follow Me!"* Whatever you do, you are responding. You may say "yes," like Matthew, and follow Christ in your life. You may say "no," like the rich young man. If you are postponing your response to the invitation, you are saying "not now." And "not now" is a "no." You must decide how you will respond to the invitation *"Follow Me!"*

The Invitation to Salvation

There is, of course, another aspect of this invitation from Christ. It is a standing invitation. It is directed not only to Matthew and the rich young man. It is directed to each and every human being. It is an invitation for you to respond to the gift of salvation.

Chrysostom notes that this invitation is an *Euangelion,* a good announcement, the proclamation of the good tidings, the gospel. This announcement, Chrysostom said, was about "the removal of punishment, and remission of sins, and 'righteousness, and sanctification, and redemption,' and adoption, and an inheritance of Heaven, and a relationship with the Son of God." This message "he came declaring unto all." It doesn't make any difference who you are, because the message, Chrysostom said, is "to enemies, to the perverse, to them that were sitting in darkness."

Why is the invitation extended to all?

> What then could ever be equal to these good
> tidings? God on earth, man in Heaven; and all

became mingled together, angels joined the choirs of men, men had fellowship with the angels, and with the other powers above: and one might see the long war brought to an end, and reconciliation made between God and our nature, the devil brought to shame, demons in flight, death destroyed, Paradise opened, the curse blotted out, sin put out of the way, error driven off, truth returning, the word of godliness everywhere sown, and flourishing in its growth, the way of life of those above planted on the earth, those powers in secure relationship with us, and on earth angels continually abiding, and hope abundant touching things to come.

It is an invitation to gracious salvation. And lest we seek to take any credit for ourselves, St. John Chrysostom added, "For not by laboring and sweating, not by fatigue and suffering, but merely as being beloved of God, we received what we have received."

When Jesus Christ extends the invitation, it is, in the first instance, to receive what God has done for us in faith and gratitude as a divine gift of salvation. Each Sunday and Feast Day we proclaim in the Divine Liturgy the redemption Jesus Christ has worked for us all and for each of us personally: "Only begotten Son and Word of God, who are immortal, and who for our salvation willed to be incarnate of the Holy Spirit and ever-virgin Mary, who without change became a human being and was crucified also, O Christ our God, and by your death you subdued Death; you who are one of the Holy Trinity, glorified together with the Father and the Holy Spirit. Save us."

As one writer recently put it, the Orthodox understanding of salvation is: "I have been saved; I am being saved; I shall be saved." Each and every follower of Christ must respond to Jesus' invitation with that understanding.

The Continuing Invitation

Our response to Jesus' invitation *"Follow Me"* does not stop with our baptism, our reception of the gift of the Holy Spirit, or our turning to God in affirming repeatedly the work of salvation He has accomplished for us.

The call to follow Christ also has particulars for the way we live our lives. Christians continually hear the invitation. It comes from Jesus Christ to each of us from hour to hour; moment to moment; when we are awake and asleep; in activity and in repose; in our family lives; in our work; in our recreation; in our financial dealings; in our relationships with government; in our relationships with fellow church members; in our inner, personal lives; in our relationships with those who love us and those who hate us.

Jesus Christ invites us to follow Him, purposefully, sacrificially, and with commitment. What accompanies the call *"Follow Me"*? Let's explore the implications by examining the accounts of the four evangelists regarding Jesus' invitation to follow Him.

St. Mark, in the earliest of the Gospel records, describes the call in this way: *"And he called to him the multitude with his disciples, and said to them, 'If any man would come after me, let him deny himself and take up his cross and Follow Me'* (Mark 8:34). St. Matthew expresses the invitation like this: "Then Jesus told his disciples, 'If anyone would come after me, let him deny himself and take up his cross and Follow Me'"* (Matt. 16:24). The word if puts the decision in our hands. We decide if we will follow Christ or not.

To whom is the invitation directed? Mark and Matthew differ slightly in that Mark describes the invitation as directed to *"the multitude with his disciples,"* while Matthew refers only to *"the disciples."* Mark's account is broader, including both the apostles and the people. Matthew's account singles out the apostles. All Christians are called to be followers of Jesus Christ, both those who lead in the Church and those who make up the body of believers. All the laity are to live their lives as followers of Christ.

In addition, Matthew's account reminds the leaders, the bishops, priests and deacons, that their responsibility to respond to the call of Jesus is even greater. The clergy, as members of the Church like everyone else, are called to personally follow Christ. But, the Lord said to His apostles *"To you it has been given to know the secrets of the kingdom of God"* (Luke 8:10) and *"Every one to whom much is given, of him will much be required"* (Lk. 12:48). The responsibility of the laity is not at all lessened by the affirmation of the high responsibility of the clergy to be models of the Christian life.

Taking Up the Cross Daily

What does following Christ mean? It means denying oneself and taking up one's cross to follow Christ. To deny oneself is not pretending that you do not exist, or rejecting your own existence, or thinking you have no value as a person. This would deny that you are created in God's image and likeness. But *it is* to deny self-will, pride, selfishness, egotism, arrogance, conceit, haughtiness, and vanity. To take up one's cross is to follow Christ's example of self-sacrifice for the sake of the Kingdom. It is another way of saying that we live not for our own self-satisfaction, but in love for God, for our neighbor, and yes, even for our own true well-being.

Or, to put it another way, Jesus says to us *"If any one serves me, he must Follow Me; and where I am, there shall my servant be also; if any one serves me, the Father will honor him"* (Jn. 12:26). If we deny ourselves we must change our priorities, just as Matthew did; one moment, looking out for "Number 1," the next, serving Jesus.

When Will You Be the Lord's Servant?

You know what these words mean! There is a choice to be made. Or rather, there are choices to be made. But when? And how often? St. Luke quotes Jesus in a slightly different way from Mark and Matthew: *"If any person would come after me, let him deny himself and take up his cross daily and Follow Me"* (Lk. 9:23).

The difference in St. Luke's Gospel is the addition of the word *daily*. So following Jesus is more than being baptized once in the past. Baptism is the beginning, and many other actions follow, marking you as a servant and follower of Christ:

* Chrismation
* attendance at the Divine Liturgy
* repentance for sins committed

* efforts to grow in grace
* reception of Holy Communion and participation in other
* sacraments (such as Holy Unction)
* forgiving someone who has hurt you
* seeking to avoid evil and do good
* giving to those in need.

All these and many more things mark you as a member of Christ's Church and as bearing the identity of a Christian.

But taking up the cross daily makes another kind of demand on you. We cannot be Christians of the past only. Christians are Christians each and every day, *daily*. The critical questions you must ask yourself every Monday, Tuesday, Wednesday, Thursday, Friday, Saturday, and Sunday are these: "Am I following Christ *today*? Am I bearing my Cross *today*? Am I serving the Lord *today*? Am I living the Christian life *today*?

Sure, you and I and every Christian, even when we try hard, often miss the mark. The Greek word for sin, is *amartia*; it literally means missing the mark. The response to *amartia* is *metanoia*, which literally means a change of mind. We usually translate it as repentance.

It is important for us to remember that St. Peter denied Jesus three times during the events of the Crucifixion. In the twenty-first chapter of the Gospel of John, the Lord asked him *"Do you love me?"* three times. With Peter's thrice-repeated repentant affirmation, Jesus restored him to his apostolic ministry by telling him *"Feed my sheep."*

This exchange of forgiveness and restoration ends with these words: *"And after this he said to him, 'Follow Me'"* (Jn. 21:19). In the same sense, every time we sin we are called to repentance; and once we repent, we too, hear the same injunction from the Lord, *"Follow Me!"*

Responding to the Call

Jesus invites you to follow Him, whatever the circumstances of your life. Under a tree, *"Jesus found Philip and said to him*

'Follow Me'" (Jn. 1:43) Wherever you are, whatever your circumstances, Jesus challenges you to put His words into practice!

"*Follow Me!*," Jesus says to each of us, to me and to you, to make our Orthodox Christian Faith a living, vital, moving force in our lives.

"*Follow Me!*," Jesus says to each of us, by joyously receiving the true faith, committing yourself, your life, your mind, your heart, your talents and resources to Him.

"*Follow Me!*," Jesus says to each of us, by living the Orthodox faith with dedication and devotion in practice and in deeds.

"*Follow Me!*," Jesus says to each of us, by sharing the Orthodox Faith with the world that needs to receive it. Proclaim the Faith to all who will hear. Present it to all who will listen. Support those who practice the work of mission throughout the world.

"*Follow Me!*," Jesus says to each of us, by overcoming separateness and narrow nationalisms to make the witness of the Orthodox faith unified and strong in our land.

"*Follow Me!*," Jesus says to each of us, and make Christianity a reality in the place you live.

You have your marching orders! Christ invites you and urges you to personally and positively respond "Yes!" to His call, "*Follow Me!*"